TAKE NO PRISONERS

TAKE NO PRISONERS

A NO-HOLDS-BARRED APPROACH
TO CORPORATE EXCELLENCE

MARVIN A. DAVIS, CTP

AMACOM

AMERICAN MANAGEMENT ASSOCIATION

New York • Atlanta • Brussels • Chicago • Mexico City • San Francisco
Shanghai • Tokyo • Toronto • Washington, D.C.

This publication is designed to provide accurate and authoritative information in regard to the subject matter covered. It is sold with the understanding that the publisher is not engaged in rendering legal, accounting, or other professional service. If legal advice or other expert assistance is required, the services of a competent professional person should be sought.

Library of Congress Cataloging-in-Publication Data

Davis, Marvin A.
Take no prisoners : a no-holds-barred approach to corporate excellence / Marvin A. Davis.—1st ed.
p. cm.
Includes index.
ISBN-13: 978-0-8144-8060-1
ISBN-10: 0-8144-8060-8
1. Industrial productivity. 2. Corporate profits. 3. Industrial management. 4. Organizational effectiveness. I. Title.
HD56.D38 2008
658.5'15—dc22

2007034439

Printing number

10 9 8 7 6 5 4 3 2 1

*To my wife, Trudy,
whose encouragement has helped me
in all my endeavors.*

CONTENTS

PREFACE

When I wrote my first book, *Turnaround: The No Nonsense Guide to Corporate Renewal*, back in 1987, corporate life was a lot simpler and I had a lot more hair. As the years have progressed, globalization has occurred and the Internet has linked the world in ways none of us ever expected. The advent of cellular technology has made the virtual office a reality, and the intensity and quality of competition have increased by orders of magnitude. Conversely, many new opportunities have emerged as a result of these factors. American industry has realized it can compete and utilize resources outside U.S. borders.

Yet as a seasoned turnaround professional I see companies making many of the same mistakes that hindered profitability in 1987. I still see failure to adapt to changing market conditions. I still see companies missing their full earnings potential by not asking themselves some basic questions or analyzing their operations properly and taking appropriate action.

In this book I revisit the basics of corporate operations and the "secrets" of the turnaround professional as he increases the cash flow and profitability of his client companies. I address market strategy and techniques that people can utilize to identify and take advantage of key market opportunities.

I discuss customer-by-customer analysis, the ability to enhance the corporate customer base, and the right time to "fire" the unprofitable customer. I address the lies that companies tell themselves so that they don't have to change or so that they don't have to admit that they are on the wrong path. I explain the investigatory techniques that turnaround consultants utilize and how in seven to fourteen days a good turnaround professional can identify most of a corporation's major problems no matter the size. I discuss the fastest methods to increased profitability and cash flow including a technique called niche pricing, which can change profitability virtually overnight. In detailed discussions of both the P&L and balance sheets, I show the reader cost-reduction steps that have worked for me many times in many situations.

In Chapter 6 I explore the optimization of the size of the organization and address the difficult task of "right sizing." I also discuss methods for motivating workforces and minimizing involuntary attrition in crisis situations.

In Chapter 13 I discuss both pros and cons of international outsourcing, the effects of globalization on the enterprise, and how to utilize outsourcing for elements of the business.

There is a discourse in Chapter 17 on how to treat your banker and how to structure personal guarantees if unavoidable. I also present the wisdom of treating your banker as you would a good vendor, including bidding his or her services out.

Finally, there is a discussion of succession planning and "monetizing" one's position, or "cashing out," in Chapter 20.

I feel that this book will be of interest to senior executives in both small and large corporations in both the private and public sector. It is full of common-sense approaches to everyday business problems that have been proved through personal experience.

INTRODUCTION

I'm a turnaround professional; that is, for the last 30 years I have been advising, operating, and fixing troubled companies. They have ranged in size from a few million in sales to multibillion-dollar companies. They have been public and private, owned by families or by equity funds, but they all have one thing in common: They were all underperforming in some manner.

In 1986 I wrote a book called *Turnaround*, which was a cookbook full of recipes that a CEO could utilize to fix his or her broken company. As the years progressed, I realized that many companies may not be "in crisis," yet are performing at suboptimal levels. So this book is a compendium of steps that I have used in real-life situations to drive favorable profitability and cash flow into ailing companies.

People often ask me what the most common problem in troubled companies is, and my response is, "Failure of management to act on changes in the environment." Or in other words, failure to recognize and act upon eight things:

1. Changes in technology
2. Shifts in the marketplace
3. Changes in marketing techniques
4. Changes in manufacturing methodology
5. Changes in the regulatory environment
6. Changes in the economy
7. Changes in internal politics
8. Changes in cost structure

1

Or in short, complacency.

The usual reaction to these changes is small, ineffective modifications to corporate performance followed by sheer panic when the problem becomes so large it can't be ignored. Ignorance of the event or management's reluctance to admit it missed a fundamental change in structure causes this behavior. The typical defense I hear is, "We thought the change was temporary and would correct itself over time."

The truth is that problems tend to become worse over time and corporations need a proactive methodology for identifying and solving problem areas early—before they become major items. In this book I identify these methods; however, the real problem is convincing management to utilize some relatively simple actions to remedy the situation.

One current problem is the cost of oil and energy, which we all know finds itself in the cost of every single aspect of American business. Energy is contained in the materials we buy, the plastics in our ballpoint pens, the cost of making steel, the cost of transporting all the materials we use, the cost of running machinery, and the cost of running air-conditioning. In lieu of a national energy policy, which doesn't appear to be coming anytime soon, companies must anticipate this problem and mitigate it by taking certain internal steps, from conservation to pricing modifications. I get into specifics in Chapter 10, but every corporation in the United States needs to recognize the problem along with specific steps to take now.

In order to utilize this book properly, one must have an open mind and a willingness to drive the process. We often say in the turnaround process that time is our enemy, but actually our enemy is inertia. I hope my series of ideas will assist you in driving your organization to ever-higher levels of profitability.

CHAPTER ONE

SETTING OBJECTIVES

One of the first steps in a turnaround and in profit enhancement is setting your short- and long-term objectives. It seems almost ridiculous to ask what the objective of the effort should be when a company is underperforming or bleeding gobs of red ink. It's like asking a seriously ill patient what he wants when he checks into the hospital. "To get better, of course," is what he'd probably say. Likewise, the client usually looks at me in disbelief and says, "Stop the bleeding!" or "Fix the problem." However, the "fix" is conditioned upon the real objectives, which may be one of four things:

1. Improve profitability and grow the current company long term.

2. Improve profitability and prepare the company for sale.

3. Improve profitability and keep the company the same size.

4. Begin liquidating the company after stabilization.

Often management has been through a lengthy period of poor performance and fatigue has set in with banks, which have been attempting to "work out" an underperforming loan for a long time without success. The desire to get rid of the loan at almost any cost becomes overwhelming. This is called "lender fatigue."

The same thing often happens to investors and management. Thus, their first response to my question about their objectives is often, "Fix the damn thing and get me out." But as one might expect, each of the four objectives I mentioned drives a different course of action.

OBJECTIVE 1: IMPROVE PROFITABILITY AND GROW THE CURRENT COMPANY LONG TERM

In this scenario, companies take steps to improve profitability and make a concentrated effort on a long-term growth plan that emphasizes four things:

1. Improving the balance sheet, including possible additional equity and lending, which will support future growth

2. Identifying and enhancing the core competencies of the company

3. Searching for a long-term banking relationship that has not been spoiled by the current problems

4. Sourcing long-term investments that companies may need to ensure continued growth

OBJECTIVE 2: IMPROVE PROFITABILITY AND PREPARE THE COMPANY FOR SALE

In this situation, you are dressing the bride for the wedding (or sale, in this case). The intent is to achieve the highest-possible earnings before interest, taxes, depreciation, and amortization (EBITDA). Because most companies are valued based on a multiple of this number, maximization ensures that the greatest value is received in a sale.

This is a legitimate exercise that I have performed many times. In one instance, I was called in to operate an outdoor-sign company because the CEO had died suddenly. I was told at the outset that my role was to help the company's managers handle the steps necessary for a sale as well as prepare them psychologically for such a change.

I asked the managers of the investment fund that owned the company, who wished to "cash out," if they minded if I "tuned up" the enterprise to maximize EBITDA. They consented, and through various actions, I managed to raise the EBITDA by $2 million annually. This translated into an additional $14 million in sales price at the 7x multiple that the new buyer was willing to pay.

To improve the prospects of selling a company, managers take four actions:

1. Absolute maximization of profit through various short-term means, including personnel rationalization, severe cost cutting, and renegotiation of all external factors including rents and loans

2. Investment only in capital projects that will yield results in the short term. Investment in a new computer system that won't yield savings for several years would be inconsistent with a "fix and sell" objective.

3. Open discussion with lenders about their intentions in order to elicit their cooperation.

4. Retention of an investment banking firm to help prepare for the sale while managers are improving the profitability.

OBJECTIVE 3: IMPROVE PROFITABILITY AND KEEP THE COMPANY THE SAME SIZE

This approach is most prevalent in private companies in which the principals wish to maintain a lifestyle without the energy and financial resources it takes to operate and grow a company.

In this instance the obvious objective is to maximize cash flow that can be returned to the shareholders. There is no desire to invest in high-risk growth alternatives. In other words, the owners want to stay within a comfort zone regarding size or industry.

There is nothing wrong with this approach. Four needs in this particular instance are:

1. Maximum profit and cash flow

2. A low-risk, market-volume maintenance plan

3. Judicious investment in high-yield, low-risk capital projects

4. Retention of key personnel through long-term incentives

OBJECTIVE 4: BEGIN LIQUIDATING THE COMPANY AFTER STABILIZATION

The last scenario is the orderly liquidation of the business. I must admit that I really don't like liquidating businesses, but sometimes fatigue becomes so great that the owners and lenders are unwilling to wait for a sale. In this instance, maximizing asset value is the only governing criterion. This means that some production may be necessary to optimize the value of work in progress or inventory.

Four key issues are:

1. Minimizing labor and other costs

2. Collecting accounts receivable

3. Disposing of assets including inventory, property, and equipment

4. Selling intellectual property

One can see that the initial assessment of goals is very important as to how one proceeds in the turnaround. Obviously and thankfully, most activities are centered on improving companies in the long term. Often I will start with the company wanting to "fix and flee," and as we are progressively successful in the turnaround process the objective becomes a "fix and grow" strategy.

BUILDING YOUR ARSENAL THROUGH INTERVIEWS

Now that you've determined your goals, you are ready to determine your company's problems and opportunities and gather ideas from those who know your company best: your employees, your customers, and your competitors.

Every consultant, as an initial step in "learning" a company, conducts a series of interviews. This is like borrowing a client's watch to tell her what time it is. Management can do the interviews, but often personnel are too frightened to be totally honest with management, so a third party such as a consultant should be utilized to gather data. Either way, interview three groups:

1. **The employees.** They work day to day in the environment and often see internal mistakes long before you do.

2. **The customers.** They are on the receiving end of your goods and services and are in the best position to tell you if you are meeting their needs.

3. **The competitors.** They are a great way to hear about "other" plans in the marketplace.

Let's revisit each of these areas.

THE EMPLOYEES

When I go into a company, management usually introduces me to all the employees and tells the employees to be completely open with me. Usually people describe my role as one of "improving profitability," which is absolutely true. I then set up one-on-one interviews with all the key employees at the vice presidential and director level as well as with many of the workers at much lower levels within the organization. I will talk to the head of the union and the janitor. I will talk to engineers and to machinists. I will talk to salespeople and sales managers . . . you get the idea. I want to get a true cross section of the company and I ask the same question of each of them: "If you were president of the company, what would you do to improve profits and make the company a better place?"

Someone once asked me, "How do you get people to talk to you?" My problem is usually the opposite one. Often I get much more information than I need or want; in other words, I can't stop the torrent of words and ideas.

A lot of times one must sit through some personal petty complaints, but more often the response is thoughtful and well considered. After about the tenth interview, a picture of the nature of the company begins to emerge. A feeling for management style and corporate culture becomes evident and the same complaints and suggestions begin to emerge from the interviews.

If a complaint appears from multiple sources, I classify it as symptomatic of a problem. If a suggestion sounds good to me, I explore it with a number of interviewees to test its validity. Of course I take copious notes throughout the process and in my notebook I place a star or asterisk next to key ideas that emerge.

I was once called in to fix a petrochemical company in Pennsylvania that had been losing $3 million per month. As part of my interview process I spoke to the head of the quality-control lab. He was a very impressive young man who had worked for the previous owner of the facility, a very well-known U.S. oil company.

I asked him about his background and he said he was a chemical engineer with a master's degree in business. It seemed odd to me that this bright light was in a role that did not reflect his background or education. As I probed further, I found that his formal education, especially the MBA, was not to the liking of the plant manager, who was an "old-timer." The interviewee said he had made some suggestions to the prior owners about cost conservation and operating methodology that would save the company over $1 million annually. He was told that if he made any more proposals of that type he would be fired and to "just do his job." I asked him to tell me his ideas, and they sounded logical and sensible. I checked his approach out with others, including other engineers, and it appeared valid. Within 48 hours of our interview, I was implementing those ideas with this young man's help. He eventually became the chief operating officer of the company and helped me save many millions more.

THE CUSTOMERS

Many companies have learned to listen to their customers through telephone interviews or feedback questionnaires. I've received a feedback form from virtually every hotel I've stayed at, and as you can imagine, I've stayed at quite a few. In the rare instances I've responded with a complaint or a suggestion, I've obtained zero feedback. I've written letters in order to provide helpful hints to Delta Airlines, Marriott, and many others with no response.

In the turnaround process, one cannot wait for response cards or attempt to get others to respond to a canned survey; one must be proactive in seeking opinions from customers. As with the employees' interviews, I talk to big and small customers, customers we currently serve, and those we have lost. And I ask the following four questions:

1. What do you like about our company?

2. What don't you like about our company?

3. How can we serve you better?

4. And for those who are no longer customers: Why did you leave us?

The answers to these questions are often enlightening, sometimes shocking, and hardly ever related to price, as one might think.

Quite often the customers' perception of the client company is completely different from how the company sees itself. Again, when a number of customers make an observation repeatedly, one begins to think that there is validity in what they're saying.

For example, I once had a customer tell me we were undervaluing a product we were selling to him. He stated that our quality was much better than the competition's and if we charged more he could easily pass the increase on to his customer, the eventual consumer. Needless to say, I was on my mobile phone changing prices before I left his parking lot.

Personally interviewing customers whom you have lost allows you to accomplish two tasks:

1. Identify the cause of the customer's departure.

2. Provide an opportunity to bring the customer back into the fold again.

THE COMPETITORS

Every company should know as much about its competitors as possible. What are they doing? Where are they going? With the advent of the Internet, you can gather a great deal of public information on your competitors; and for public companies, their 10Ks and 10Qs are available.

But two of the best methods of finding out about the competition is through your sales network and by asking your competitors for information! What do I mean by this? When I am at a convention I always visit my best competitor's booth and make a point of meeting with the CEO of the competitor. Obviously avoiding some questions that might get me into legal difficulty, I do ask the following: "You are a great competitor—to what do you owe your success?"

One would be amazed at the answers I get. Often ego takes over and I get a description of how my competitor plans to approach the market and with what products and services. At worst I get an idea from merely observing the products and services it is pushing.

★   ★   ★

Now you have an idea of where you eventually want to take your enterprise, some ideas about the problems and opportunities, and some ideas about how the business can be modified to begin generating cash. Extract what you have found from the investigation and place the information in a key "problem area/symptoms" list for action later.

CHAPTER TWO

COMMON LIES COMPANIES TELL THEMSELVES

I have seen great ideas wither and die because companies tell themselves lies that are ingrained in their corporate makeup, and thus they fail to fix problems. This is why one of the biggest problems in optimizing a company's profitability is not external (unless the market strategy is extremely flawed). It is the culture of the company.

So what are these lies?

"WE'RE SO MUCH BETTER THAN THE COMPETITION, WE DON'T HAVE TO WORRY"

This is corporate chutzpah or arrogance. IBM, General Motors, and Ford, all major companies with great resources, fell into this trap. They underestimated their competitors and took their eyes off the ball. IBM failed to realize that it was not "keeping up" with more agile companies in the PC market and lost its position through sheer arrogance.

Ford, GM, and other U.S. carmakers failed to see the strategic steps of the Japanese carmakers, failed to understand the Japanese carmakers, failed to understand the consumers' desire, and have lost tremendous share to offshore companies over the last 50 years. Toyota is now the largest auto manufacturer in the world, but Ford and GM are struggling to stay alive. I will revisit the Ford and GM problems since there are many other problems in these companies. But at many points in their histories these companies have been poster children for Arrogant Corporation Syndrome.

For example, I was once being interviewed for the board of one of IBM's "enterprise" businesses. The business had developed a new method of creating DVDs, was about to go into the DVD publishing business, and professed to be seeking guidance in this area. During the interview I asked how IBM was picking titles, because I saw the enormous potential of information flow, through the computer, of this new medium.

The thing to remember in all of this was that the people who were running the enterprise were all born and bred IBM "techies." They stated that they were picking titles without any outside input and were selecting titles that appealed to them individually and that they believed the market would accept. In addition, IBM was afraid to lend its logo and name to the new enterprise, so they had to come up with a separate logo for the effort.

I think their first interactive DVD was about the sex life of the tsetse fly or something equally interesting. Of course I'm being facetious, but I told them they were doomed to failure because of their arrogant approach. I told them they needed to view themselves as publishers, not as IBM, and pick products with mass appeal. Second, they should arrange to utilize IBM's considerable brand recognition in their marketing.

Needless to say I didn't make it onto the board and the venture disappeared, much to my chagrin.

"OUR PROFITS ARE SO GOOD THEY CAN'T BE IMPROVED"

Many executives are reluctant to reexamine their profit structure for fear of embarrassment if they discover an overlooked area of profitability. I can't name the number of times I've been told that an area is doing the best that it can and I should seek profit enhancement elsewhere. This slams the door on investigation, on structure modification, on pricing, and on other areas of improvement. The only way to get past this is to:

- Convince the affected executive that you are going to make a hero out of her if she will let you look.

- On a less desirable basis, have the CEO force the issue.

The facilitator in this instance must have the full support of those in command and the indication that there are no protected areas or sacred cows that are beyond scrutiny. The ideal is to have a team that bands together to achieve common profitability goals. Quite often I have had to replace people who were not receptive to this concept and continued to be obstructionists.

"OUR BUSINESS MODEL IS AS GOOD AS IT CAN POSSIBLY BE"

One of the major exercises I go through in every company I help is a reexamination of the business model to determine if it is flawed in any way.

Quite often a company will be marketing to the wrong customers or selling the wrong product or service. It would be like opening a pork rib joint in a highly religious/kosher or Muslim neighborhood. It just wouldn't fly. I have also found companies selling to the least profitable part of the market just because it's "easier," or selling to buyers because of the high volume they will take despite the fact that the business is at an extremely low profit level. It is amazing how many companies invest money, people, and time in flawed or suboptimal ventures.

For example, I was once the CEO of a wax-refining company that was losing many millions of dollars per year and had been doing so since its inception. The initial marketing concept for the company was to sell microcrystalline waxes to a small but high-priced user market (pharmaceuticals, food, etc.). In concept this top 5 percent of the business would more than cover the cost of the other 95 percent the company would sell at breakeven or a loss or burn for energy.

There was only one small problem: Since microcrystalline waxes have an enormous impact on the physical characteristics of the products in which they are used, extensive testing at great cost would therefore be needed to introduce a new source of these waxes. In addition, quantities of microcrystalline waxes used in any single product were miniscule. In view of these factors, no level of pricing incentives could convince end users to switch from their existing suppliers to us. The probability of selling product was nil. In Chapter 3, I talk about what I did to solve the problem, but what I had was a severely flawed market strategy. This was after more than $100 million had already been invested in assets.

"OUR PRICING MODEL CAN'T BE IMPROVED—BESIDES, WE'RE CHARGING THE MAXIMUM WE CAN GET"

When I tell my clients that I always get a price increase that adds to profits, I always get a mixture of disbelief and horror. Most companies fight price increases like a virulent disease because they fear a loss of volume. The greatest resistance to price increases, no matter how well thought out or benign, is internal.

In this book I will illustrate through various techniques how every company, with few exceptions, can drive dollars to the bottom line through pricing. I have never failed to achieve price increases for a client successfully unless internal resistance was so great that it was unwilling to take a chance.

This area is the most frustrating for me because it takes so much to achieve. At one company I was involved in, it took almost a year and many meetings to achieve a price increase that the entire company endorsed.

"OUR COST STRUCTURE IS THE OPTIMUM IT CAN BE UNDER THE CIRCUMSTANCES"

No one likes to admit that there is a better or cheaper way to do something. I have seen companies pay as much as twice the going rate for a service or product because it was difficult or inconvenient to obtain competing bids or because of prior relationships. The U.S. Government is a prime example of purchasing inefficiency in action. Of course companies must strike a balance among price, quality, and delivery, but often the worst offenses in cost structure occur when there is no regular review process. In one company, by merely reviewing the manner in which we insured our facilities and casualty insurance we saved $1.2 million per year in premiums.

In this book I will discuss most major cost areas and some devices to lower costs; however, the caveat is that all costs must be continually reviewed to determine if they can be further optimized.

"OUR ORGANIZATION IS SO GOOD THAT I (THE CEO) DON'T HAVE TO BE INVOLVED ON A DAILY BASIS"

A sure sign of trouble exists when the CEO or any executive thinks that he can operate the business on autopilot. I was recently involved with a small private company whose president had a passion for sailing. His business was failing, but rather than face the problems, he would find any excuse to leave and sail. It was obvious that he hated the process of fixing the business and was escaping into his hobby because he couldn't face day-to-day problems.

I have also seen executives who think that operations are doing so well that they don't have to monitor or control the company. Both approaches are equally faulty. Companies need controls in place and need guidance from someone who has a vision of the future. Companies can operate for a short while without daily leadership but soon begin to falter when the strategic guidance begins to falter. The Walt Disney Company began to falter when Walt died. It was a local joke that the corporation was being managed by WWWD (What Would Walt Do). It wasn't until new visionary leadership stepped in that the company began to grow once more.

"OUR ORGANIZATION IS AT ITS OPTIMAL LEVEL"

A question I ask participants in my various seminars is, "If you had to discharge someone in your organization today, who would it be?" There is always a name associated with the response, which proves to me that almost every organization is suboptimal in nature.

Keeping an organization "right sized" is one of the most difficult tasks a manager can perform, and often this painful process is delayed because of emotional issues associated with the process. Most companies have taken the "easy" method of offering early retirement or block reductions in staff based on longevity. These methods are faulty because early retirement denudes the knowledge base and block layoffs get rid of high-energy, high-potential individuals.

In Chapter 6, I will discuss a scientific and logical method for adding and reducing personnel that is dependent upon talent and need rather than pure numbers of people.

"COMPLACENCY IS NOT A PROBLEM IN MY COMPANY"

Complacency is the enemy of all companies and avoiding it is an everyday job of every manager. When a company becomes complacent, it has begun to slide down the slippery slope of failure. If anything, the speed of communications—e-mails, Internet, and fax—has made the cost of complacency more severe. I don't know about you, but I find that I must work even harder to keep up and keep ahead of events that affect my markets and my business.

"FRAUD IS NOT A PROBLEM IN MY COMPANY"

It is estimated that fraud plays a major role in fully 50 percent of business failures. I must admit, having been CEO of over 100 companies, I have found fraud in some form in each of them. It is especially true in troubled companies, since someone in the company wants to "get theirs" before the ship sails. The lessons of Enron, WorldCom, and Tyco have exposed all of us to fraud and waste in the corporate arena. In Chapter 18, I will discuss how to detect fraud and what to do about it. I will discuss some things employees don't consider theft but really are. I will also show how to empower the organization to deal with fraudulent behavior on the part of employees, including senior executives.

"MY BANK LOVES ME"

For some reason most companies and executives elevate their banking relationship to that of an amorous affair. Maybe because it involves money. I hate to disillusion my readers, but your banker is a vendor who sells you money and charges you for the privilege in the form of fees and interest. Like any other vendor, he or she should be treated well and kept informed of the company's performance; however, he or she should be measured against other vendors of the same type. In Chapter 17 we will discuss the care and feeding of your banking relationships, how to treat personal guarantees, and how to have fallback positions in case your banker fails you.

★　★　★

Now that we've examined the lies companies tell themselves, let's look at the reasons why companies don't reach their full profit potential.

These are the 12 deadly failures of management:

1. Failure to recognize changing market conditions and act on them

2. Failure to resolve internal conflicts and resistance

3. Arrogance

4. Overspending during good times

5. Failure to continually rationalize the organization

6. Failure to act on substandard performance

7. Inability to think "outside the box"

8. Failure to delegate

9. Failure to define market strategies

10. Failure to demand implementation of marketing plans

11. Failure to tie compensation to corporate performance

12. Failure to plan for the cash needs of the business

These failures spring from some of the lies companies tell themselves, plus mistakes that I will discuss later in the book.

One of the toughest things for a manager to do is to continually self-review his decisions and actions to determine if he is falling into the traps that these twelve failures represent.

As you read through this book, and as you make decisions on a daily basis, refer back to this list and ask yourself honestly if you are guilty of any of them. Then consider using the techniques and solutions I present to work through the problem.

One thing that I do that may be helpful is to take a few quiet moments at the end of each day to be introspective and ask myself if my actions truly reflect the principles of management that I espouse, or if I have lapsed because of inertia or other distractions. The key to good management is the ability to be self-critical enough to admit mistakes and correct emerging problems.

CHAPTER THREE

MARKET STRATEGY

One of the biggest errors a company can make is to embark on a new market strategy that is not valid, or if carried to its logical conclusion, unprofitable. I mentioned the wax company that was founded on an irrational marketing premise and into which many tens of millions of dollars were invested before the basic concept was disproved. It really took a very minimal amount of investigation to determine what the correct approach should be and it would have saved a lot of effort and extra cost if the investigation had been performed prior to the formation of the company.

Many market strategies are like Athena, the Greek goddess who was born full grown from the head of Zeus. They magically appear from the heads of senior management without much further or deep investigation and get adopted because they sound good.

There are three points at which new market strategies are adopted, and one should be cautious at these points or nexuses in corporate growth. These are:

1. New ventures (the underlying strategy for formation of the business)

2. New products or new markets for an established company

3. Responses to competitive expansion or a shifting
   marketplace

It sounds almost silly that a corporation would adopt a product
without thorough examination of the potential market or without
optimizing the channels through which the product is introduced
to the market, yet this happens often.

I was once involved with a company that "cloned perfect
plants." The process included developing a "perfect" plant
through hybridization and then "cloning" the perfect plant in a
sterile facility through the use of growth hormones and a very
labor-intensive manufacturing process. In other words, the company used a very expensive process to create an exact copy of the
"parent" plant. When I asked the CEO of the company what he
was cloning, he stated, "Household ferns." I asked, "Why household ferns?" He replied, "Because they are the easiest." Now, one
must realize that household ferns are sold at very low prices
through grocery stores and the big-box stores such as Costco and
Wal-Mart. It was apparent that the ability to recover value from
the products and channel of distribution chosen was minimal.
There had been no analysis to determine where to get maximum
value from the marketplace, which reflected the exacting effort to
create a perfect plant. In other words, the company had been operating (at a loss) for five years without any value-realization potential.

By modifying the strategy to one in which perfect plants were
critical, cloning was meaningful, and through which we could
charge enough to recover all operating costs plus a profit, we
changed the paradigm of the business.

MARKET ANALYSIS

You must ask yourself, "Am I in the most profitable section of the
marketplace?" or, "Am I expending a great deal of effort on mar-

ket segments that will never yield the kind of returns I am searching for?"

The reason many companies, even large ones, don't do the analysis is pure arrogance—the feeling that they know the market better than anyone else (i.e., "Please don't bother us with the facts. Our minds are made up.").

The investigation process takes effort and research—but not as much as one might think. The process is called "slicing and dicing" the market. In Figure 3-1, I have a sample format for slicing and dicing by laying out the various markets for the product or service you plan to offer.

The template has five elements:

1. The market or end use for the product or service

2. The global current sales volume in dollars for the product or service

3. The average profit margin realized currently in the market segment

4. Who the competitors are

5. The growth rate of the market sector

Let's discuss each in turn.

MARKET OR END USE

This briefly describes the place or channel that offers the product or service. For example, in the case of the petroleum waxes we were attempting to sell, some typical markets were:

1. Candles

2. Fire logs

3. Blenders (or converters)

4. Food and chemicals

5. Waxed paper

FIGURE 3-1 ■ The Slice-and-Dice Sample Format.

Rank	Market/End Use	Size $	Average Margin	Competitors	Growth Rate + or –
1					
2					
3					
4					
5					

* Data Sources *

1. Trade publications
2. Competitive data
3. Literature
4. Market studies
5. Surveys

Each of these has a physical set of needs and various distribution channels that can be quantified.

I have operated apparel companies and learned that besides the men's and women's markets, there are subcategories including sportswear, casual, and formalwear, as well as various types of distribution such as large discount chains, specialty stores, department stores, and Internet retailers. Each of these had volume and margin structures that needed to be examined in view of the products we were capable of producing.

The mere act of defining the market options a company has at its disposal often identifies missed segments that the company should be taking advantage of and currently is not!

People can identify market segments by examining trade publications and literature, looking at competitive data, getting input from the sales force, or conducting formalized market studies and even surveys. A few years ago the Internet was not a factor in the market and now it is a major channel for direct sales for many companies. In the future, new markets will emerge that we can't even conceive of today.

MARKET SIZE

Once a market is identified, its global sales volume in dollars must be quantified. Quite frankly, extremely low-volume markets tend to be overlooked unless there is a compensating high level of profitability. And sometimes very low profitability offsets high-volume markets. The key to this exercise is to identify target markets when the combination of volume, size, profitability, and potential is optimal.

MARKET MARGIN

Each market segment has its own profitability. Obviously this is as important as volume. It often makes sense to attempt to pursue lower-volume, higher-margin markets and utilize your resources primarily in this pursuit.

COMPETITION

Before entering a market, one needs to examine the competition and its strengths. The competition represents resistance and must be considered as part of an overall market decision.

GROWTH

Most companies want to invest in growing rather than static or decreasing market segments since an investment in a growing seg ment may yield growing sales opportunity.

★   ★   ★

By laying out this strategic analysis in quantitative form, you are preparing a market shopping list that allows you to prioritize the key markets you wish to pursue. You may find after this analysis that you are diligently pursuing the worst markets from a gross profit standpoint or ignoring the highest-growth markets with the greatest potential. Because markets change over time, it is best to perform this analysis at least annually.

SIMPLIFIED MARKET PLAN

There is a second necessary analysis that relates to the cost of entry into the chosen marketplaces in order to determine the eventual yield of the venture to the corporation. I call this analysis the simplified market plan (see Figure 3-2). It takes the market segment you have chosen and becomes more specific as to the people, capital investment, and time it will take to reach market. You now can calculate the profit potential to the company as well as the return on investment to see if a market is worthwhile financially.

FIGURE 3-2 ■ The Simplified Market-Plan Analysis Template.

Market Description	Size	People Cost	Investment	Time to Market	Expected Sales/Year	Market Share	Potential Profit/Year

Surprisingly, few companies go through this kind of analysis and certainly they almost never revisit strategic market decisions that they made in previous years until decreases in profitability and sales force them to reevaluate their positions.

In the case of totally new products or ventures, the same rigorous analysis can be performed, but the inputs are less certain. Test markets can prove the premises of the market strategy in certain instances, but it is still valid to go through the analysis in order to know what one's expectations should be.

In certain businesses, companies can test their new strategies on a small scale before launching them on a full-blown basis. In a retail environment where stores already exist, we can try a new marketing model out in a few "test stores" and track sales to see if we have a successful idea. Food companies commonly will test-market products in limited markets prior to a full rollout. All of this may seem overly cautious, but as we all know, the cost of a mistake can be high!

I have often gained great profits for companies by identifying the point in the marketing chain where the greatest profit is made. In the case of the petroleum wax company, the "slice and dice" of the market showed that the greatest return on investment occurred at the formulator level. We sold certain waxes wholesale to formulators that would mix them with additives and sell them to specialty end users at very high profits.

Thus, the formulator was making gross margins three to four times what we were making, and with minimal investment on the formulator's part. In fact, it was leveraging off its market knowledge to obtain far superior profits than ours. Our answer to this dilemma was to acquire a formulator; thus, with the source of product and the new knowledge of markets, we increased our profitability considerably.

In the case of the plant-cloning facility, we discovered through the strategic market analysis that most of the profit in the distribution chain was made by the secondary grower, which grew the cloned plant to a size that was salable at retail. The secondary grower was gaining the greatest return for a relatively small investment. By merely keeping plants longer in the growth cycle, we doubled our profitability and shortened the distribution chain to the eventual buyers.

Once you have a strategy that you feel works and is optimized, the next step is to optimize your customer base.

CHAPTER FOUR

THE CUSTOMER

One of the most valuable assets of a company is its customer base. Customers are the *raison d'être* (reason for being) for a company. Essentially, a symbiotic relationship exists between a company and its customer base: You nourish customers by providing goods and services that they need, and they nourish you by providing the funds that a company needs to survive.

Yet many times companies get into relationships that are destructive to one or both parties. It is ironic that often companies don't even realize that they are dealing with an unprofitable client. An example of this is a small advertising agency that was in a downward profitability cycle. The agency had been covering its losses through borrowings from an especially tolerant bank each year. Upon examination of its customer base, the agency discovered that the local arts alliance (which represented the symphony, theater, etc.) composed 40 percent of the agency's business. The agency was charged with assembling the program booklet for the symphony and theater and obtaining the advertisers in the program. Theoretically the volume of advertising in the program was supposed to cover the cost of designing and printing the program. Due to the extensive effort in obtaining advertisers, which was outside the normal scope of my client's services, the net effect was a loss to my client annually. In other words, he was digging a hole from which he would not be able to emerge.

Because the arts alliance provided 40 percent of the advertising agency's business, the owner was absolutely in terror of surrendering the client. We formulated a plan to turn a liability into an asset. Because the arts alliance loved the ad agency's design, we had a platform from which to operate. We put together a proposal that let my client continue to design and print the programs at a price that would allow him a reasonable profit and move the responsibility for obtaining program advertising to the alliance itself. We knew that there were other agencies that would compete for the business, but the relationship was good and the client liked the product. We also had a plan for modifying the overhead structure of the business in the event that we lost the alliance and the 40 percent of the agency's business it represented.

Fortunately, the alliance accepted our proposal and the business began digging itself out of the onerous debt structure. We also formulated a plan to reduce the arts alliance business from 40 percent to 15 percent of the sales by increasing non–alliance-related business.

CUSTOMER-BY-CUSTOMER
PROFITABILITY ANALYSIS

Many companies do not know what percentage of their profit comes from which customers. I have been amazed by what a customer-by-customer profitability analysis has shown me. This kind of analysis helps answer the following questions:

- What is the margin I receive from each customer?

- Is the customer covering my variable costs?

- Is the customer covering my fixed costs?

- Is the customer contributing a profit?

- Am I expending effort on a customer who is growing? If not, is it better directed elsewhere?

- Can I improve my profitability on this customer or do I need to say "no thanks"?

- Am I overengineering my product or service to this customer?

In Figure 4-1, I provide a template for a customer analysis.

The analysis identifies the customers, what they buy, the fixed and variable costs of what they purchase, and the gross profit from those purchases. Also, the analysis accounts for the cost of "other support," such as free freight, special discounts, special warranties, cooperative advertising, and placement premiums. The obvious objective is to obtain a net pretax profit on a specific customer and what he or she purchases. As I stated, I have never failed to be amazed at the results of such analysis. Often the customers who I think are my best are in reality among the worst.

An example of this was a large-volume big-box chain whose demands were great but which could offer my client, a manufacturer of sports apparel, extremely high volumes of sales. Its approach was to order several thousand dozens of product in the exact color and size assortment that it needed. In addition, there was a date certain for delivery. We had to sew the retailer's label onto the product and attach specific hang tags that contained its pricing and bar codes. We also had to provide the product on hangers, ready to hang in the stores. This chain's stated condition of doing business was payment 60 days after delivery of goods.

Since my manufacturing operations were integrated back to thread, we would spin the thread, weave the greige goods, dye the fabric, cut the material, sew the goods, sew in the specified labels, put on the hang tags, assort as required, put the goods on hangers, and ship the goods by the agreed-upon date. Sometimes, near the shipment date, this large customer would "decrease" the order because "sell through" of the product had changed as the fashion demand for our product had changed. We would then be

FIGURE 4-1 ■ Customer Analysis Template.

Customer	Products Purchased	Sales $	Var $	Fixed $	$ Profit	Other Support	% Profit on Sales

forced to dispose of this excess inventory in a secondary discount market.

Through the customer profitability analysis, I found that the cost of all the special services we offered the large retailer, combined with occasional product refusal and long payment terms, put this customer's profitability well into the red. It was especially hard to make the decision to drop this customer because of its volume. The competitive nature of the industry did not allow for price increases significant enough to cover the cost of doing business, so we decided to wind down sales to this customer over time while reducing overhead, including the closure of one facility, and redirecting our sales to more profitable channels.

In another instance, I was forced to oversee the liquidation of a company that manufactured a critical component for an automotive company. The component was a very precisely manufactured technical family of products and was the sole supplier for the automotive manufacturer. Over the years the automotive company had squeezed the component manufacturer for price concessions to the point where there was no profitability. After several years of losses, the investors and the bank were facing "lender fatigue" and wanted out of the company. I was given no option but to liquidate a 100-year-old business that might have been saved had the company performed a customer analysis at an earlier date when other options were still available.

FIRING A CUSTOMER

The hardest thing a company can do is fire a *customer*. There are reasons for doing this besides obvious economic ones. These can include the following six things:

1. Overly demanding service requirements

2. Consistent slow pay and collection problems

3. Exaggerated warranty demands

4. Continual threats of legal action

5. Quality requirements beyond reasonableness, coupled with high returns

6. Abusive or dishonest relationship

Firing a customer, as I have illustrated, can actually be a constructive process and should not be an emotional decision. It should involve the following four steps:

1. Determine what the economic cost of the customer is in real dollars. Quantify each service and demand of the customer, and determine what you must charge in order to recover these costs.

2. Have a frank discussion with the customer to determine if you can modify its demands to make doing business together worthwhile, for example, agreeing to more acceptable payment terms.

3. Raise prices and put the continuance decision into the customer's court.

4. Prepare your organization for the loss of business by reducing overhead.

Because customers can actually drain profit rather than generate profit, companies should perform customer analyses often, perhaps every six months. Sales conditions and product mix change. With a new customer I recommend a review of the account's performance after the first three months of service. This simple review will often avert a great deal of angst in driving continued profitability for your company.

CHAPTER FIVE

PRICING

If you read and implement no other chapter in this book, make it this one. The reason I place so much emphasis on pricing is that I have never failed to find a pricing opportunity at a client company. It is the single most rapid method of increasing profitability available to a company. The effect on cash flow can be virtually instantaneous, and it does not require a change in manufacturing methods, company structure, or painful cost cutting. If done correctly, it will have little or no effect on sales volume.

The methodology I use focuses on those niches where there is a significant price disparity. For example, most companies raise prices in response to external events such as inflation, fuel increases, and raw-material price increases. These increases are usually "across the board" and often come too late to stay ahead of the cost curve. I propose a completely different approach that reflects the value of each good or service offered.

I warn you as we start on this exercise that the greatest resistance to pricing increases is usually internal rather than from the consumer. Sales people hate it when prices increase, because it causes greater resistance to the sales process. Over the years, I have learned to restrict salespeople's discretion over discounts dramatically. This is because sales personnel for the most part will immediately move to the lowest price structure available when quoting the customer. I have even found *myself* giving volume discounts to customers who can never achieve the mandated volume, and I have competed with imaginary pricing in the marketplace.

Across-the-board pricing is difficult to implement because it is obvious; it relies on the competition to follow, if it is to stick, and almost always causes some adjustment in volume. If you are selling a commodity such as wheat or soybeans, pure competitive factors determine pricing, but my methods apply to virtually everything else.

The reason niche pricing is not applied in most businesses is that it takes work, must be utilized often, and takes a real internal "selling" process if it is to be effective.

COMPETITIVE PRICE ANALYSIS

To find out if a price increase is justified, and to gather the data to convince your skeptics, I suggest that you perform the following two analyses:

1. Competitive pricing analysis (see Figure 5-1)
2. Competitive advantages and disadvantages analysis (see Figure 5-2)

The first of these, the competitive pricing analysis, recognizes that the marketplace is the real determinant of the price of a product or service.

In order to get started, you must compare the price of the product or service you offer against the competition's. You should compare pricing on a product-by-product basis or equivalent service offered with three other competitors' products. Companies can obtain these data from sales personnel, customers, and distributors. As you can see from Figure 5-1, you need to get not only the selling price of the competitor's product but also the various discounts competitors may offer. For example:

FIGURE 5-1 ■ The Competitive Pricing Analysis.

| Product | Cost | Selling Price | Discounts | | | | | | Net Price |
			Freight	Terms	Volume	Co-op	Warranty	Other	
Mine									
Competitor A									
Competitor B									
Competitor C									

F I G U R E 5-2 ■ Competitive Advantages/Disadvantages Comparison.

Product	Competitive Advantages	Competitive Disadvantages	Comments
Mine			
Competitor A			
Competitor B			
Competitor C			

- Is there free freight or is the product free on board (FOB) the plant? In other words, who pays for the freight, you or the customer?

- What kind of payment terms are there, and is there an early payment discount?

- Is there a volume-discount structure?

- Is there a cooperative-advertising allowance or shelf-space allowance?

- Is there a warranty on the product or service, and what is its value?

- Are there any other discounts to pricing?

Your product may have the highest list price but due to various discounts may have the lowest net price.

I have also included a column in Figure 5-1 for cost. You may have to guess a competitor's cost, but doing so accomplishes two things:

1. It may indicate whether your cost structure is out of line compared with the competition.

2. It may identify products or services that are losing money.

Cost should never be a determinant in setting price; the marketplace is the sole determinant.

"Now," you might say, "I've got 500 or 1,000 different items [stock keeping units—SKUs] that I offer, and this exercise will take forever to do!" In most instances I have been able to perform this analysis within four weeks, no matter what the size of the company. Obviously I start with the highest volume and profit contributors first and work my way down to lower-volume products. In one company, I had over 32,000 SKUs to analyze and we performed the task in three weeks.

COMPETITIVE ADVANTAGES AND
DISADVANTAGES ANALYSIS

The second part of the analysis is equally important, and that is an analysis of the advantages and disadvantages of the products.

How many times have you had a sales manager tell you that you must meet a competitive bid that is ridiculously low, and investigation of what is being offered you finds that the competitor's product is made of plastic, has less than half the features of your product, and offers no warranty, whereas your product is made of stainless steel, is full featured, and has a one-year warranty? When performing the analysis shown in Figure 5-2, you must be brutally honest with yourself and measure the true advantages of your product or service compared with others.

Having done the analysis, you are now ready to look at niche pricing and those spots within the spectrum of your pricing where you are not achieving payment for the true value of the product or service offered to the customer.

PRICING CASE STUDIES

In the case studies that follow, I illustrate how I have utilized pricing analysis to increase pricing and profits at various client companies.

CASE ONE
THE DISTRIBUTOR

A $1 billion in revenue distributor of auto parts located in California had almost 32,000 items scattered in 10 warehouses throughout the state. The company was having serious cash flow problems. Its customers were garages and jobbers located throughout the state. The company sold non–OEM (original equipment manufacturer) parts intended for repairing all types of vehicles. In concept it was similar to NAPA Auto Parts but sold only to wholesale purchasers.

When I informed our sales force that we were going to raise prices through niche pricing, I was informed that I was insane (a common complaint). I was informed that because of our purchasing power we were able to buy products at the lowest possible cost, but our suppliers often provided suggested retail price to our customers and thus we were caught in a margin trap between our supplier and our customers with no room to move unless our suppliers let us.

I asked how often the customers were updated on pricing and what items were covered. It turned out that only the pricing on the highest-volume items (antifreeze, shock absorbers, batteries, etc.) was updated weekly. I asked how many items were in this category and it turned out to be a mere 6,000 SKUs. The other 26,000 items we had in inventory were slow-moving items (such as a distributor for a 1967 Mustang and an engine block for a 1937 Chevrolet), which made us a full-service warehouse company. I then asked how the company priced these "C" and "D" (slow-moving) items. The sales managers said they took a large markup of 100 percent at the time of purchase and also added a charge to reflect company carrying costs.

I then posed a hypothetical situation to the gathered sales managers: Imagine yourself as the owner of a 1937 Chevy. You have restored this automobile and drive it periodically every Sunday. One Sunday it begins to sound strange and you take it to your local mechanic. The mechanic informs you that you have a cracked engine block. You now have three choices:

1. Contact General Motors for a replacement block, wait several years, and eventually pay an enormous amount for it.

2. Take the car home and convert it into a planter on the front lawn.

3. Call our company and have a new engine block within
    24 hours.

I then asked, "What is the value of the engine block that we have
in inventory?" The answer was that the value to the customer is
close to the total value of the car. By keeping this philosophy in
mind, we then repriced all the slow-moving but distinctive items
in inventory. We raised prices on some items as much as 1,000
percent depending on their utility and distinctiveness. We examined every one of the 26,000 "C" and "D" items in inventory.
The net effect due to the low velocity of these items was a 4
percent overall annual increase in pricing. Four percent of $1 bil-
lion in sales is $40 million. The effect on sales volume was unde-
tectable, and the $40 million went a long way toward helping the
company out of its cash flow dilemma. ■

CASE TWO
THE JEWELRY COMPANY

I was asked to assist a very large, public, retail jewelry chain in
acquiring a sizable competitor that happened to be in bankruptcy.
In the process of assisting with the acquisition and rationalization
of the combined companies, I observed that the profitability of the
new parent was less than it should be. Management was extremely
cooperative and receptive to new ideas, so I proposed that we
perform a niche-pricing exercise. The competitive price analysis
revealed that a smaller nonpublic company was charging much
more for products of similar quality and design.

We then began to push the pricing envelope by asking our
buyers and merchandise managers to "push up" the pricing on
new and distinctive items of jewelry. We began to meet strong
resistance from all levels of management and were given dire pre-
dictions of lost sales and missed profit goals.

In order to overcome this, we set up a demonstration program
to show that jewelry for the most part is a "blind" item and that

pricing is more dependent on a combination of store reputation, product design, and economic conditions than on gold or precious-stone content. We placed a number of items of jewelry in a room with no pricing and then asked company personnel to give us a proposed selling price on each item. The variability between low and high estimates was over 500 percent. We then moved the pricing decision to the office of the president and began using "pricing panels" to maximize the value equation. Profits of the company soared while volume stayed at the same levels. The company was public and its stock price tripled. ■

CASE THREE
THE VITAMIN COMPANY

One of my earliest successes in pricing was a vitamin company located in the northeastern United States. The company had a gross-margin problem and my task was to get its margins up immediately. The company produced high-quality natural vitamins that were sold through health food stores. Because the problem was gross margin, I either had to lower the cost of goods, or raise pricing, or both. The company formulated and encapsulated its own product and imported various vitamin-bearing substances from around the world. The company also bottled its own product. Very fortunately the owner of the company owned health food stores that sold both the company's and competitors' products; thus, a comparative price analysis was easy.

The company sold 600 different vitamins and vitamin formulations. We initially classified the 600 into three categories:

1. Combinations of vitamins in which there were no obvious competitors (approximately 200 items)

2. Products in which there were limited competitors (approximately 200 items)

3. Products that were essentially generic (approximately 200 items) for which there were many competitors

The company had the advantage of being "all natural" and of recognized "high quality." In the process of analyzing pricing on a per-pill basis we discovered that the absolute maximum retail price a customer would pay for a bottle of pills was $55 at retail or approximately $27 at our wholesale price to the store selling the vitamins.

We vowed that we could never go over $25 at wholesale for a bottle of pills and would vary the number of pills in the bottle to ensure that this wouldn't happen. We then looked at category one and decided that we could raise prices 20 percent without affecting volume. Again we varied the number of pills in a bottle to bring the price in line. With regard to the products where we had limited competition, we found that the competition was charging almost identical prices on a per-pill basis; however, we determined that the "natural" feature of the product and the quality reputation of the company were worth a 5 percent increase in price.

In the case of the generic products, we found that we were slightly overpriced (2 percent) and were losing money on 50 of the products, so we dropped the losers and lowered prices where appropriate. The net effect of all this was the equivalent of an 8 percent overall price increase with an increase in dollar sales volume due to the recognition of optimal package size. ■

CASE FOUR
THE AUDIO PUBLISHING COMPANY

In 1985 I actually published my first work with Nightingale-Conant in audio format. It was called *The Profit Prescription*. I had a lot of fun recording it, and as was the custom, I had lunch with Vic Conant, CEO of Nightingale-Conant one day. Vic indicated that Nightingale-Conant was having some real financial problems as a result of increasing talent costs and other reasons. We decided that I would do a quick survey of Nightingale-Conant and make some recommendations.

I called the entire staff together at some point in my investigation and asked a very simple question: Why are you charging $39.95 for albums that add so much to the quality of your customers' lives? The answer was simple also: The price had been set many years before by Lloyd Conant, Vic's dad, and no one had ever changed it.

That was enough for me, and we began to modify pricing based upon the perceived value of the message imparted by the album. I think we increased some albums to $99.95 and some to over $150. It took four months, but the company became very profitable. My last album, published in 2002, is called *The Turnaround Formula* and is on both CD and tape and retails for $500.

I have tried to illustrate the power of pricing in this chapter. Every company, no matter how big or small, has pricing opportunities within its structure. It takes real intestinal fortitude to force the pricing initiative. The niche pricing does not have to be overt or obvious. By unbundling products or services and charging separately for them, one can often obtain pay for services that were taken for granted.

In consulting, quality is often equated with price. In other words, the more you charge, the more your advice is valued. This is the secret behind branding and the ability to charge for design. Each reader should reexamine the pricing criteria within his or her own organization and examine those criteria using the methods of analysis presented here. Just remember you will always have an internal fight and resistance. Persevere—it's worth it! ∎

PEOPLE

I have been running and advising companies for over 40 years, and my faith in the importance of having a good team within a company has been reinforced time and time again. We can all call to mind recent events, in both the private and public sectors, where incompetent or undertrained management has caused a situation to become worse instead of better. As a former partner of mine stated, you need "superstars" in game-breaking positions. This becomes especially acute when a company faces a crisis or if a company is small and each manager strongly influences the performance of the company.

The ancient saying "the fish stinks from the head" is very true. In other words, key managers, especially the CEO, determine the intellectual, moral, and operational tenor of a company through their demeanor, words, and actions. For example, it is difficult to believe that the Enron debacle could have happened without tacit approval and encouragement from management in its overzealous pursuit of monetary goals without regard to the ethics of what it was doing.

In this chapter I discuss some simple techniques that will help any company and any manager obtain maximum productivity from people while keeping morale high.

KEEPING PEOPLE INFORMED/COMMUNICATING

When I am called in to a company, things are usually a disaster. The company is losing money, the operations are in disarray, and people at all levels are demoralized. The very first thing I do is call everyone in the company together and tell them why I am there and what the goals and objectives are for the company. I do this through a series of large corporate meetings with all the personnel, from top to bottom. I physically go to each operating location to deliver the message and receive feedback from the people at that location.

Any corporation can utilize this very same technique to continue to drive the organization forward. By holding quarterly reviews at every operating location and giving a "state of the company" message, one can create an atmosphere of teamwork very quickly.

There are some rules of "engagement" that need to be communicated prior to these sessions. They are:

- Ensure that you will be absolutely candid and truthful in your communications and will attempt to answer all questions from the employees unless you don't know the answer or the answer is confidential and would not be in the best interests of the company to discuss in an open forum.

- If you don't know the answer, you will attempt to place an answer on the company bulletin board within 24 hours of the meeting.

- All those present should remember that any discussions or disclosures should be considered confidential and "kept in the family." This is especially true in public companies, which have legal requirements for public disclosure.

At these sessions each employee should have a 3- by 5-inch card on which to write questions he or she wants answered. The employee does not have to sign his or her name. This allows shy or fearful people the latitude of asking tough questions without fear of recrimination.

A typical session would have the following eight agenda items:

1. An overview of the last quarter's operations, both successes and failures

2. A discussion of how well the company is meeting its goals for the year

3. Special thanks to individuals who have done a good job

4. Recommendations to the staff and personnel as to where they can improve (e.g., quality and service issues)

5. New goals for the forthcoming quarter

6. Personnel changes within the organization

7. Awards for service or special monetary incentive awards

8. Questions from the troops

You will be amazed and delighted by the input you will get from this process, and the ability to hear and fix operating and tactical problems "on the fly" in a timely manner is exciting.

As a result of sessions like this, I have discovered simple solutions to issues that have caused quality, productivity, and service problems. For example, at a quarterly meeting of a company that manufactured highly complex electronic and mechanical devices, we discovered that one of our vendors was providing a product that was at the low end of our specification range, thus making it difficult to assemble our products and slowing our productivity. The product was indirectly causing service problems, as well. The problem was not acute enough to raise the normal red flags but was indeed a problem that could become much more serious. Rapid action with the vendor solved the problem quickly.

OPTIMIZING THE ORGANIZATION

One of the questions I often ask groups of CEOs I speak to is, "Has anyone ever felt that he or she fired an underperforming person too soon?" The answer is normally, "No, I fired him six months to two years too late."

The ancillary question is, "If you had to fire someone today for nonperformance, who would it be?" Usually everyone can name someone. So what does this tell us? It says that all of us want to give our employees a chance to prove themselves. In family-owned companies, there are additional complications of relatives who are feeding from the company trough and may or may not be contributing to the company's welfare in proportion to their compensation, or may be, in a worst-case scenario, hindering corporate growth.

So how does one determine who is necessary to the organization and who is not? How does a company downsize in times of market shrinkage without losing its key people?

We read daily of corporate downsizing based on length of service, early retirement, or a whole series of other methods that have nothing to do with addressing the needs of the company other than reducing cost. I contend that these methods are absolutely destructive to the company in the long term. There is, however, a methodology that works. It is called the "green-field" approach and I have used it very successfully for years. It consists of annually reviewing the organization to determine what the organization should look like given the constraints of growth and corporate need.

It works best if one writes the various positions of the organization on Post-it® notes and places them in the appropriate positions in the organization chart along with small descriptions of each position. One should avoid placing names on these positions or creating a position just to employ an individual (as in the case of some family companies). In a separate place one should name all the individuals in the company. Then with each position one should ask the key question: "If I were filling this position today with the most competent individual I can, who would it be?" Often it will not be the person who is in the job at present.

This process is called the green-field approach because you are starting with a virgin, green field and are rebuilding the organization based on need and competence. This approach, if used properly, identifies who is necessary to the organization and who is not. It identifies newly created positions that are not essential to the organization and conversely it identifies functions that need to be filled for the company to grow.

The only problem with the green-field approach is that it does not consider union agreements, which usually call for a seniority-based "pecking order." When positions are reduced, however, I have found that a union will grant certain concessions if the company can make a persuasive enough case with regard to "critical" individuals.

Under normal circumstances, all companies should do a green-field analysis on an annual basis and every six months when there are large changes occurring in the marketplace.

In my business I go into companies, conduct the analysis, and am faced with a "Friday Night Massacre" in which I am forced to reduce staff and personnel by hundreds, if not thousands, of individuals. If an annual review occurs on a regular basis, there may be small changes in personnel but nowhere near the massive changes we have seen in corporate America in the last few years. Adverse conditions do not happen overnight. It often takes many months or even years, and it is the reluctance of management to act on these conditions (see Chapter 1) that leads to massive reductions in force.

The normal approach for large corporate reductions has two components:

1. Early retirement reduces force by incentivizing the older (more highly paid) individuals to leave the company, but it also destroys the skill base of the company without focusing on the individuals you need to keep.

2. Conversely, seniority-based layoff programs get rid of the brightest and most energetic employees who represent the future of the company.

The solution is neither. It is green field that allows you to select according to the needs of the organization. It is admittedly easier to develop broad "all-encompassing" plans, and they are much easier to implement, but it is similar to cutting off your foot because you have a hangnail.

In family businesses, green-field analysis works especially well because it identifies the functionality (or lack of functionality) of family members who are part of the business, and it identifies who should no longer be part of the active business.

MOTIVATING EMPLOYEES THROUGH INCENTIVES

One of the best ways to motivate a workforce is through the use of incentives to recognize extraordinary performance. Incentives break down into several categories. These are:

- Financial incentives

- Recognition awards (such as rings, plaques, etc.)

- Rewards, trips, and status awards

Each one of these is effective in its own way and may be combined to provide the proper motivation for your staff and operating personnel.

Let's look at each in turn.

FINANCIAL INCENTIVES

These are cash bonuses tied to the performance of the company, a division, or an individual. Of course, there is an infinite number of ways to structure bonuses. Once corporate or individual financial goals are set, attaining 90 percent of the goal should start yielding payouts to individuals. The caveat here is that the goal should be a realistic stretch for the company, say last year's performance plus 10 percent. These goals are usually set through the budgetary process and should be based on net gains of the corporation.

I like to utilize bonus programs as retention programs as well. I recognize the bonus amount each year but stagger the payouts equally over three years; thus, if the employee quits prior to the end of the three years, he or she loses the unpaid portion of the bonus. If the employee is terminated, the bonus is paid in full. These, in effect, become golden handcuffs for the employee.

The important thing about any financial incentive is that the goal setting be an interactive process in which the employee has input. The greatest disincentive is to set unattainable goals or for employees to miss goals several years in a row.

RECOGNITION AWARDS

Many times incentives need not be financial but rather a ring or a plaque that recognizes the employee's effort and contribution. One of my greatest thrills in business has been to receive "recognition" gifts from the companies I turned around. I have an office full of objects companies have given to me. I have an upside-down and backward clock given to me by a company in Australia for helping it "down under." I have a Jim Bowie knife in recognition of cost cutting performed at one company, and I have a plaque with a plastic doughnut on it in recognition of the many doughnuts I consumed while fixing one company. I also have a brass plaque depicting the rear end of a horse for my being a "horse's a-- " in saving another company. You get the idea. Many times these items, combined with financial awards, can go a long way toward welding company loyalty and providing a way to celebrate successes.

REWARDS, TRIPS, AND STATUS AWARDS

Another very effective way to motivate employees at relatively low cost is to provide incentives such as trips and dinners. These incentives include the entire employee's family in the motivational process. Some examples that I have used are:

- A special trip for the employee and spouse to a resort location

- A gift certificate for dinner for two at a local restaurant

- A gift certificate for merchandise

- The lease of a special luxury automobile for one year

- Membership in a special "president's club," which involves dinner with the CEO or another key executive, and tickets to sporting events

Again, these tend to stay in the mind of the employee long after the event has occurred. The important thing about incentives is that they must be varied each year to keep them interesting and vital.

When I was in the navy, in the "iron men and wooden ships" era, I was an officer in charge of the weapons-system radars and computers (missile fire control) for our missile systems. Since I was financially limited as to what I could do for my men to incentivize them to keep some highly complex and somewhat experimental systems in operational shape, I decided to utilize their pride to drive the equation. Because we had two missile systems, I divided my crews into an A and a B team. I also indicated that for each firing we would essentially have a contest and then use the system that was tracking best and providing the steadiest computer solution for the missile firing. This decision was always made just as we were about to shoot. I promised the winners a beer party when we went ashore if we used their system.

I knew that I had motivated the men when I caught several of them sneaking back from shore leave early to maintain and tune up their systems. This beer–party incentive cost a certain young lieutenant junior grade a lot of his rather meager pay, but we received the Navy "E" for excellence three years in a row and a number of commendations for performance.

PERSONAL COMPLIMENT

What is perhaps the greatest incentive of all doesn't cost a cent: It is the honest verbal recognition of a job well done. An "attaboy" or a heartfelt personal compliment from one's supervisor often goes further to engender job satisfaction than any other method. We are all quick to criticize but very slow to compliment or to say thank you to those who have done well. The pace of business and the use of e-mail tend to bring a sterile quality to personal communication.

★   ★   ★

As a final reminder, performance-based compensation, especially in public companies, is becoming the key determinant in overall pay plans for executives. Stockholders are forcing compensation committees to consider the growth and profit performance of a company when considering key executive compensation. There have been several situations where stockholder lawsuits have arisen out of improper compensation. I think that performance-based compensation is not only just, but is good for the company in the long term.

CHAPTER SEVEN

CONTROLS

It is said that in the very earliest of airplanes, the pilot often became disoriented in adverse weather and had to rely on the pressure on his rear end to determine if he was upright or in a
turn—hence the expression "flying by the seat of your pants."
With the advent of high-speed sophisticated aircraft, today's pilot
has to rely on input from a myriad of onboard computers and
instruments to keep him on course and able to react, in time, to
potentially adverse conditions.

Today's business is like a supersonic or even hypersonic aircraft. The contemporary executive needs input from a variety of
sources to keep the company on course, often utilizing sophisticated computer-based tools to provide adequate warning signals
of impending dangers. In this chapter I am going to discuss some
simple tools and techniques for making sure that you are able to
achieve your goals and hear more important alarms and "look-out
signals" that tell you that something is awry early enough to take
action. These "controls" include benchmarking, cash control,
control by walking around, and an action plan. Remember, one
of the early no-no's discussed in Chapter 1 is the failure of management to take action in response to changing market or operational conditions. These controls will help you stay abreast of the
situation and prepared to address any changes.

BENCHMARKING

One of the best controls a company can use is benchmarking. Benchmarking is merely comparing your corporate performance against others in your business, especially those companies you consider successful.

This concept is very helpful because it compares how you are doing as a corporation with another company that is in your type of business and has approximately the same business obstacles to overcome. Note, however, that no two businesses are exactly alike and one should keep this fact in mind when comparing numbers.

There are many books about benchmarking techniques, but I will give you some key performance methods that you might utilize.

SOURCES OF BENCHMARKING INFORMATION

These sources can often provide comparable data that you can utilize to measure your own performance.

- Public filings (10Ks, 10Qs, annual reports, press releases, etc.)
- Internet articles
- Sales personnel
- Trade associations
- Credit reports
- Trade publications
- Offering memoranda

Let's briefly examine each source in turn.

Public filings.   It is much easier to obtain comparable data on public companies. You can obtain 10Ks and 10Qs online from the Securities and Exchange Commission. The only problem with public filings is that companies may be consolidating divisions that are not comparable and may distort the comparative data; however, with a little rational thinking you can usually obtain close approximations of the numbers you need.

Internet articles.   I am continually amazed by the information I can glean about competitors from the Internet. Often business magazine articles expose data on companies that would not be available otherwise. The Internet will lead you to the appropriate publication.

Sales personnel.   You can often glean a great deal of information from your own sales personnel or distribution channels about the sales and growth of competitors, as well as their profitability.

Trade associations.   Trade associations often compile comparative data on companies from surveys they perform. They will provide these data to you if you are a member. The data are often not identified by source but are very useful and are usually classified by corporate size.

Credit reports.   By tapping into the various credit-reporting agencies, you can often get some of the data you need as well as information about the financial well-being of the various players in the industry.

Trade publications.   Trade publications often write articles that provide helpful data about your competitors. If the comparative company is large enough, there may be articles in the *Wall Street Journal, Business Week, Industry Week,* or any other general business publication. Search engines on the computer can lead you to articles on the target companies.

Offering memoranda.   This one is a bit trickier than the others, but if your competitor has ever been for sale, there may be an offering memorandum (called "the book" by investment bankers) that describes the competitor in great detail. These memoranda are controlled through the numbering of copies and confidentiality agreements, but you would be amazed at how many competitors' "books" I have seen over the years.

DATA USED FOR COMPARISON

When mining sources for information, be sure to collect the following data. Then you can insert the information into the chart provided to perform a benchmarking analysis.

Sales.   Obviously you want to know the competitors' sales volumes and growth rates so that you can see if you are growing as quickly.

Cost of Goods and Gross Margin.   Obviously the competition's cost of goods and the resultant gross margin are very valuable data points to have. They immediately tell you if your production costs and/or your pricing is out of line, and they indicate if there are steps you may be able to take to maximize your gross margin. Many companies think that their performance is just fine until the cold light of comparative data illustrates that they are growing at half the rate of the market or that their gross margins are 5 percent less than the others.

Operating Costs.   Often it is difficult to obtain specific operating costs for competitive companies; however, if you can obtain the data in the aggregate, it tells a great deal about the overhead structure of the competitors. Some key overhead numbers that you may be able to obtain, however, from the sources I identified earlier are:

- Number of personnel in the company and sales per person

- Annual advertising budgets
- Annual legal expenditures

Operating Profit.   This number excludes the capital structure of the company and is a lot more indicative of performance than a net profit comparison, which may include interest payments and other items that tend to distort the comparison.

Net After-Tax Profit.   I just noted that the net profit number is not as meaningful for comparison purposes because it can be distorted by interest, capital structure, and a myriad of other factors. But it can be very informative as to your competitors' debt structure, cash needs, and tax structure.

Earnings Before Interest, Taxes, Depreciation, and Amortization (EBITDA).   The best comparisons indicate how well companies generate cash. This is why EBITDA—or essentially cash flow—is a very good comparison.

Other.   If you can get balance sheet data, you can compare the following data:

- Accounts receivable (and days of sales outstanding)
- Accounts payable (and days of payables outstanding)
- Amount of debt
- Accumulated depreciation and amortization

The format of the benchmarking analysis would look something like what is pictured in Figure 7-1.

You now have a guide to which areas may need further examination in order to optimize performance. Obviously it is desirable to meet or exceed the performance of the best of the comparable companies. I usually ask companies to perform this kind of analysis at least semiannually so that they can take action in a timely manner to correct areas where they are straying in comparison to those in their marketplace.

FIGURE 7-1 ■ Benchmarking Template.

Item	My Company	Competitor A	Competitor B	Competitor C
$ Sales (000s)				
% Sales Growth Annualized				
$ Cost of Goods (000s)				
Cost of Goods as a % of Sales				
Gross Profit $				
Gross Profit as a % of Sales				
Operating Costs as a % of Sales				
Salaries				
Benefits				
Advertising				
Insurance				
Other				
$ Operating Profit				
Operating Profit as a % of Sales				
Interest as a % of Sales				
Taxes as a % of Sales				
$ Net Profit				
Net Profit as a % of Sales				
EBITDA $ and % of Sales				
Total # of Employees				
Accounts Receivable in Sales Days				
Accounts Payable in Cost Days				
Inventory Value as a % of Sales				
Bank Loans Outstanding $				
Other				

CASH CONTROL

One of the first ways a turnaround specialist takes control in a company is to insist on personally signing all checks or authorizing all expenditures before they are paid. Now, I don't advocate doing this on a continual basis, and it is certainly difficult to do this in a very large company. However, there is no better way to identify how a company is spending its money.

In my career, I have discovered many instances of waste, and occasionally fraud, when requesting detailed expenditure reports. Some typical things I have found through this methodology are:

- Overordering of materials in order to get volume discounts without regard for our cost of capital

- False reporting of overtime in order to "pad" paychecks

- Overtime that has become institutionalized instead of being eliminated

- Failure to obtain competitive bids for key components and services (I also discovered fraud in the form of kickbacks)

- Inflated expense accounts and nonessential travel

Let's call this an expenditure-review process. At first blush it looks a lot like micromanagement, but there is no better way to get a feel for where the dollars are going in a company.

I also ask the accounting department to provide a year-to-date expenditures list, or general ledger, ranking all expenditures from highest to lowest so that I can examine the most significant areas of cost first. There is no sense hunting for pennies while leaving dollars unexamined.

It is amazing to see what comes out of the woodwork when you start questioning items you don't understand or feel may be excessive. Every manager needs to do this on a regular basis because corporations tend to become sloppy in the way they manage expenditures over time.

I will discuss the purchasing function in Chapter 15, but turn-around experts utilize incentives in the purchasing area, which can drive savings up to 3–7 percent of the cost base.

It is obvious that in people-intensive businesses, the highest costs are salaries, payroll, and benefits, and these are the first areas to question and attack. In manufacturing companies, often material costs are the key, so that's where you start!

It seems overly simple to point this out, but many times in attempting to improve profits, companies focus on the wrong areas and spend inordinate amounts of time and effort on fixing the wrong problem.

CONTROL BY WALKING AROUND

The best managers I know walk through the operations and talk to people on the job on a regular basis as a method of learning what's really going on. A good turnaround manager can walk onto a factory floor and just by feeling the pace of activity can tell you in a matter of minutes how efficient the operation is. Just for fun, go into your office or onto your factory floor and count how many people are actually working, compared with nonproductive activity. You will be amazed at how low the number is.

Next, walk around and ask random personnel the following questions:

- What are you doing?

- How are things going?

- What do we need to do to help you do your job?

- Do you have any questions that I might answer?

You will be astounded by the amount of information you will garner in a single visit. I found that one visit to the office floor or the plant operations would yield 10 to 20 actionable items that would represent potential improvement. Even in extremely large operations, I ensure that I visit each of the operating locations once a month and "walk and talk" at headquarters once every day that I am there and not traveling. This process accomplishes two objectives:

1. It points out specific areas where the operations can be improved.

2. More important, it points out to personnel that you care about them and their work. It makes management real and approachable.

AN ACTION PLAN

The fourth method of control, the action plan, is deceptively simple yet is one of the most powerful management tools I have employed as an acting CEO.

In consultation with CEOs and senior managers, the complaints that I hear most often are:

- "I can't get people to do what I want them to do on a regular basis."

- "Projects are always late and above budget."

- "In the rush of everyday operations, many tasks are lost or deferred."

- "People complain that they are overloaded and can't prioritize projects."

The action plan solves all of these complaints while providing a method of coordinating the operations of all the departments in the company. Figure 7-2 is a template that you can use to help implement your plan.

A typical action plan consists of several elements.

FIGURE 7-2 ■ Action Plan Template.

Opportunity	Action Needed	Who	When	Comments/Priority

OPPORTUNITY

What is the opportunity for corporate improvement? For example, there may be an opportunity to raise prices through niche pricing (see Chapter 5) or an opportunity to reduce insurance costs through competitive bidding. On a grander scale, there may be the opportunity to acquire market share through the acquisition of smaller competitors. You get the idea. Usually in any given company I can identify 40 or 50 distinct opportunities that it should be working on at any given time.

ACTION NEEDED

After opportunity is a column for the types of action needed to take advantage of the opportunity. For example, under the niche-pricing opportunity, the items would be:

- Perform comparative price analysis

- Perform competitive advantages/disadvantages analysis

- Determine and raise prices

WHO

The next column lists the individual designated to perform or be responsible for the action item. It is very important that this be an individual, not a group, because in order to get things done there must be an individual who is responsible for the task and answerable for its performance.

WHEN

The next column provides the driving force for the action plan. It is a date by which the task will be complete. I view this date as a contract between you and your subordinate. Thus, both parties must agree upon the date. Usually I find that people tend to underestimate the length of time it will take to complete an assignment. I often add weeks or months to the completion date. I tell the person assigned to the action item that once a completion date is set there is only one excuse for missing the assigned date, and that is "a death in the family—yours." Of course, there are all sorts of reasons to miss a date. For example, if the exercise is not possible for some reason and management is made aware of that, then an individual may be excused from the task. But no task is ever terminated without discussion.

I generally review the action items on the list once a week at my staff meeting and discuss progress leading up to completion. At that meeting we will delete action items that are complete and add new ones to the list. We will also prioritize tasks as immediate or urgent, midrange, and long range in the comments column. I review the entire task list with all the members of the staff because often the person responsible for the action item must solicit the help of others on the staff in order to achieve timely completion.

The action list provides a solid direction for any company, and there can be no question as to what people and divisions should be working on. As a turnaround consultant, I may be advising as many as four companies at the same time, but by using the action plan, I know where we are in each of the companies at any point in time.

The next question is, What do you do with a person who constantly misses his "due" dates, either through lack of ability to perform or through passive-aggressive behavior? The answer is the obvious one: You ask him to leave the organization because he, by his actions, is undermining the entire profit-enhancement process. This is often called the "sacrificial firing" because you usually don't have to do it more than once. In general, the rest of the staff members take their assignments very seriously after the company asks the first person to leave.

Again, the action plan is one of the most powerful tools that can be utilized in driving a company forward. It takes discipline to use and even more discipline to continue using over time.

For those readers who want to take time off for brief periods or take vacations, the action list provides a worry-free method for knowing that significant problems are being solved in your absence. In addition, the action list allows superperformers in the organization to show what they can do in terms of on-time and completed tasks.

The really exciting thing about the action plan is that managers at all levels can utilize this same methodology to drive action in their own departments, and it works, no matter what size the organization.

CHAPTER EIGHT

GROWTH

One of the most exciting and fun areas of corporate life is overseeing and driving the growth of a company. It is also one of the most dangerous activities a company can partake in, because if done in an uncontrolled manner, it can destroy a company. Turnaround people are often called in to solve the problems of uncontrolled growth and sometimes to bury companies whose growth plans and strategies were flawed.

As we all know, there are two types of growth: natural growth and growth through acquisitions. But it is important to remember that all growth requires cash—cash to support increased levels of inventory, cash to support increased receivables, cash to support capital and personnel increases.

INTERNAL OR NATURAL GROWTH

Natural growth comes from normal market dynamics. Growth of the business as you penetrate new markets, develop new products, or take market share from competitors composes the majority of this type of growth.

The risks associated with this type of growth relate to the internal investment needed to achieve the growth, such as:

- Additional people and their support costs
- Capital investment in office space and machinery
- Additions to the balance sheet, such as inventories and receivables

ACQUISITIONS

The acquisition of products or companies that enhance your current market position is perhaps the fastest way to grow, but this also has its own inherent risks. These are:

- Ensuring that you are paying the "right" price for the acquisition
- Ensuring that your acquisition is accretive to the profitability of your company in the long term
- Ensuring that you have a corporate structure in place that maximizes growth and profitability after the acquisition
- Ensuring that you have sufficient working capital to move the combined entity forward in the marketplace

I'm not going to discuss all the due diligence that is necessary when acquiring a company, but I am going to discuss methods that can save untold grief when growth comes from internal or external sources.

WHEN SHOULD I INVEST? AND
HOW SHOULD I DO IT?

First, always have a plan for growth. As I indicated before, growth requires cash. The very worst thing you can do is be forced to limit your potential growth in a "hot" market for your product or services due to lack of cash. By creating a plan of what it will take in terms of investment in people, inventory, and equipment, you will be prepared to line up sources of cash in advance of the growth. Bankers love to lend to growing companies with great profit potential, but only if those companies have a "plan." How many companies do you remember that ran out of cash and died because they failed to support unconstrained growth? In the turn-around business we often see companies like this.

In a growing company, there are several ways to invest so as to minimize risk. One of the methods is called the "rubber band theory of expansion" (see Figure 8-1) because you can always "bounce back" from such investments.

The vertical axis in Figure 8-1 represents dollars and the horizontal axis represents time. The upward sloping line labeled "Total Sales" represents the sales of a growing business. But sales come from two types of customers, especially in a rapidly growing market. First there are "old customers," whom you know and whom you have been dealing with for some time. I presume you know

FIGURE 8-1 ■ The Rubber Band Theory of Expansion.

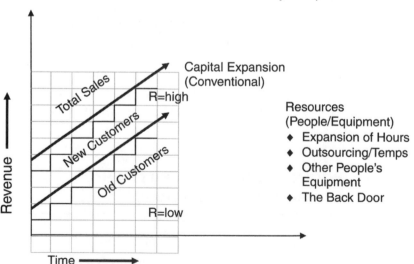

their purchasing patterns, the way they pay, and their reliability. In other words, you can quantify the risks associated with doing business with them. Therefore, the risk associated with old customers tends to be low.

The solid line labeled "Old Customers" and the area below this line represents total sales to these customers. The sales above this line, and hence the area between old customers and total sales, come from new customers. Even though they may hold great potential, you don't fully understand them yet. You don't know them and don't have firsthand experience as to their buying patterns or their payment patterns, you don't know how deeply their commitment to you as a supplier goes, and therefore the risk with these new customers is high!

Therefore, when expanding, it is always best to minimize risk. Most companies expand in a stepwise fashion because it is hard to invest in a partial machine or a part of a person. This is why investment is shown as a step line in Figure 8-1. Expanding to meet the needs of total sales is risky due to the new-customer component of total sales. So how should we expand?

I suggest that my clients consider expanding to meet the needs of the low-risk, old customers since those sales are more stable than sales to new customers. But obviously we want to meet all customers' needs or we lose them! So what can we do to close the risk gap and satisfy everyone? Here are things you can do to cover the higher-risk portions of your business.

OUTSOURCE PRODUCTION OR SERVICES

Many industries have learned to "spread the risk" by outsourcing or supplementing production both domestically and offshore. I will discuss outsourcing as a method of production in Chapter 13; however, companies can use it as a stopgap to cover ups and downs in demand, although there are risks. In short these are:

- Vendors must be carefully chosen to maintain quality standards.

- Goods should never be drop shipped to the customer from outsourced vendors unless you want to create a new competitor.

- In the case of offshore vendors, advance payment in the form of a letter of credit is often required. Thus, requirements planning is imperative.

Toy producers, which are in one of the most volatile markets in the world, have been spreading risk for years—by subcontracting most of their production to outside vendors.

Outsourcing can be applied to people as well. Hiring temporary workers is a low-cost method of expanding your workforce without long-term commitments.

EXPAND YOUR HOURS

Expanding hours simply means getting "more" out of the existing staff. Most people work at an efficiency level of 50 to 60 percent. Through discussions of need and possible output incentives, you can often get a 20 percent increase in short-term output from the existing workforce. In addition, the use of overtime or increased shifts can allow elevated levels in output at minimal risk. There are some risks associated with this approach as well. These are:

- Overstressing the staff with a heavier workload

- Institutionalizing overtime as a "normal" part of production

- Creating inefficiencies that naturally occur as part of shift work

USE OTHER PEOPLE'S EQUIPMENT (OPE)

In the world of manufacturing, failed businesses create a large market for used or surplus equipment. If you have ever been in the position of having to sell surplus equipment, you realize that the selling price is usually 10–20 percent of its "new" value. I contend that if you are unsure of a marketplace or of a customer, it is much better to purchase used equipment to satisfy that need than make a major capital investment for the "latest and greatest" equipment. As the market develops you can always purchase more efficient, latest-generation equipment to meet your production capacity. In this way you can get a 20–50 percent discount on what equipment would normally cost, and you can always sell it if the customer or market doesn't work out.

FIND THE BACK DOOR

Every really good manager considers the "downside" of any transaction or venture he or she enters and always has a "game plan" in his or her back pocket to use when and if things go awry. To this end, the back door is an operating philosophy I use when negotiating operating agreements such as leases for space and equipment. Quite simply, it is a way of escaping a "locked in" multiyear leasehold by exercising an escape clause. In a typical space lease, using the back door would mean paying the value of the unamortized lease improvements plus six months to one year's rent to the landlord. A back door can be utilized for equipment leases as well.

The time to negotiate a back door is when the lease is written and the landlord is anxious to obtain your business. It is virtually impossible to renegotiate a lease once you are in a facility or are using the equipment.

To that end, bankruptcy's one major advantage is that it provides an opportunity to reject or renegotiate executory contracts, which consist of leases among other things. So by creating back doors, one is enabling a company to survive downturns in economic conditions without the pain or cost of bankruptcy. This is important, because in my experience, companies that need workouts seem to have three events in their recent pasts: (1) they have leased new office space or production space, (2) they have just purchased new computer systems, and (3) the market has taken an unexpected downturn.

For example, I was giving a seminar some time ago to a group of CEOs on the subjects covered in this book, and one of the participants suddenly excused herself and left the room. When she came back she was very apologetic but stated that she owned a large travel agency. She had just obtained a significant corporate customer who was going to double her business. As part of gearing up for the new client, her company was leasing new facilities and adding more personnel to staff. After hearing my talk, she decided to moderate her plans and use a combination of overtime and temporary staff to cover the new client. She also was modifying her lease to contain a back door.

About four weeks later the Gulf War occurred. Corporate travel decreased virtually to zero during that period of time, especially international travel. I received a phone call from her indicating that my "rubber band theory" had saved her from bankruptcy and she was able to cut a deal with her landlord because of the back-door escape clause in her lease.

GROWTH BY ACQUISITION

There are several dos and don'ts that one must keep in mind while in the acquisition process. These simple reminders will keep you out of trouble.

DO THOROUGH DUE DILIGENCE

This is obviously the most important part of an acquisition. The use of seasoned professionals in analyzing the finances and operations of a company is essential in this step. Scrimping on professional help often leaves items unexposed, which can have a long-term effect on profitability. Investment bankers, financial analysts, lawyers, operations specialists, and real estate valuation experts are some of the people you will need. The best way to stay out of trouble is to study the company thoroughly and know all its warts along with its attractiveness. Especially troublesome are things such as unfunded pension liabilities and pension plans as well as executive contracts and leases. These are called legacy items.

BUY "ASSETS ONLY" IF YOU CAN

If you purchase the equity of a corporate entity, then you inherit the liabilities along with the assets. Unfortunately, for this very reason most companies are unwilling to sell assets only. They don't want the problems associated with disposing of what is left behind. If you are buying a company out of bankruptcy, you can often leave the liabilities behind and take only the assets you wish—if there is a sale or you present a plan. There may be competition for the sale in a bankruptcy scenario.

PREPARE A PLAN AND STICK TO IT

The biggest failure among companies that grow by acquisition is failure to prepare a rationalization plan and/or failure to integrate the acquisition. When you acquire a "like" business, there are often duplicate overheads, facilities, positions, and various items such as insurance plans and computer systems. There should be a plan prior to the actual acquisition of how to handle duplication and which areas and people are going to be eliminated as a result of the merger of the two entities. I have helped many companies adhere to merger plans that were abandoned after the deal was done due to the pain associated with integration.

Ideally you want to end up with the best features of both companies, including the best people resources. Companies can make the people decisions by utilizing the green-field approach, mentioned in Chapter 6, for the combined entity. In any case, it is absolutely necessary to drive the plan. Many rollups of similar businesses fail because of poorly defined merger plans.

SOME "WATCH OUTS!"

Some nontraditional and hidden areas to watch out for in acquisitions are:

- Long-term potential cash obligations that are not exposed on the balance sheet, such as potential litigation or understated warranty obligations

- Unfunded pension liabilities and other liabilities related to personnel, such as retiree benefits

- Insurance "tails" related to self-insured plans where not all claims have been filed

- Unreported inventory and excessive receivables shortages in value or aging

- Change-of-control triggers in corporate contracts, which can cause large cash payouts to executives and vendors

- Fraud of any sort

I don't mean to scare you with these items, but having been in the turnaround business and having been involved in a number of fraudulent-conveyance lawsuits that lasted for years, I tend to be overly cautious. There are books about how to acquire companies, and they give details on how to investigate and purchase companies; however, the best thing to do is employ the experts I mentioned in the "Do Thorough Due Diligence" section.

In almost every transaction, there is a "holdback" of a portion of the purchase price to cover minor items not accounted for in the due diligence. If there is suspicion of any problem, this holdback can increase from its normal level to as much as 35 percent of the purchase price.

So the key points to avoid future growth-related problems are:

- Prepare a plan for growth through either natural growth, acquisition, or both.

- Determine the sources of cash you are going to use to fund the growth.

- Use the rubber band theory to minimize risk.

- Have an alternate plan to recover if a method of growth does not work.

- If you are acquiring a company, use adequate professional help in the due diligence process.

- Prepare an integration plan and stick to it!

- Create an adequate "holdback" of the purchase price.

CHAPTER NINE

KEEPING THE BALANCE SHEET BALANCED

In a troubled situation companies are always hunting for cash and use the balance sheet as a source of cash that may not be readily available from a lender. In a nontroubled company, there is a tendency over time to get sloppy with balance sheet items such as receivables, payables, and inventory, which can be "milked" to reduce loans or provide cash for other endeavors, such as growth or reducing debt. Companies are often reticent to be tough on these areas because once they are tight there is a need to keep them tight to avoid using cash once again. There is also a reluctance to reduce old inventories due to the P&L loss effect of writing off old or obsolete inventory in a timely manner.

The steps I am going to describe are real actions I have taken in companies to raise cash, and I employed them because there was no choice. In a healthy company it takes impetus and a considerable amount of nagging to get some of this done, but the payoff is well worth the effort.

CASH

Large companies usually have a treasury function to maximize the investment of cash and near-cash funds. Often this same function does not exist in smaller companies. The potential gain on short-term deposits is often lost due to lack of a short-term investment program. It's like having a great deal of cash in your non-interest-bearing checking account instead of in an interest-bearing money market account. Your best source of short-term investment advice is your banker.

I was on the board of a small company whose chief financial officer (CFO) was reluctant to use overnight investment vehicles due to the large fluctuations in the business's cash needs. At one point we had almost $2 million sitting in accounts at suboptimal interest rates. If one thinks about it, a one percent difference in interest rate on $2 million can generate $20,000 annually. In a small company, this difference can mean a great deal and it is pure pretax profit. Examine your cash policies to ensure that your cash is working for you.

ACCOUNTS RECEIVABLE (A/R)

Most companies, large or small, are terrible at managing receivables. In most instances companies carry a receivables balance of 45 days or more. Companies that sell to the government or have international sales carry A/R as long as 120 days even though their stated terms are 30 days. Large big-box retailers are notorious for negotiating long payment terms from their vendors.

So how do we shorten the time before you get your cash? Again, in troubled situations when bank loans are difficult to get, A/R is a great source of cash. There is no reason why your A/R shouldn't be close to the terms of sale. Here are some tips.

SET YOUR TERMS OF SALE PROPERLY

Typical credit terms are 30 days; however, many companies require deposits prior to beginning work. I am on the board of a company that builds highly specialized stainless steel equipment to the customers' specifications. In this particular company we collect 50 percent of the sale price at the time of the order and the balance at the time of shipment. Because of the highly volatile cost of materials and the engineering effort required to make the product, it is imperative that we obtain the deposit so that we can purchase materials and "lock in" our costs.

Most companies are also lax about the way they construct their sales documents. They fail to provide for a penalty (typically one and a half percent per month of the outstanding balance owed) if the invoice is not paid on time. Also, more important, they fail to include in their sales documents *the ability to recover collection costs.* The cost for collection of an account, especially if you must use an outside agency, is between 30 percent and 50 percent of the amount owed.

You may never use the penalty or collection-costs provisions of your sales documents, but they provide you leverage with customers who are consistently late with payment. A provision in the sales documents for binding arbitration in the event of a dispute can save high court costs when trying to collect from a dissatisfied customer. A great many companies have moved to binding arbitration as a method of dispute resolution. You should consult a good attorney in preparing this critical sales document since local or state laws often govern terms.

In dealing with the U.S. Government, often a small discount, say 0.5 percent net 10 days, can get you paid rapidly. The government is mandated to take advantage of any discounts offered; thus, an invoice with time limitations on discounts goes to the top of the payment pile.

When dealing in offshore sales, one must realize that foreign corporations are used to paying slowly or on different terms (usually 60 to 90 days) than U.S. companies, and delinquent accounts are extremely difficult and costly to pursue in foreign courts. The answer to this is to require irrevocable letters of credit drawn on a U.S. bank as a precondition of sale.

Of course, overriding all of this is the creditworthiness of the client and the competitive credit atmosphere.

MAKE EVERYONE A COLLECTOR

I believe that the best way to keep A/R low and in line with terms of sale is to make everyone a collector. In most companies the A/R clerk calls the accounts payable clerk at the delinquent company to get it to pay. This very seldom works. I like to elevate the process for delinquent accounts so that nonpayment is a problem for everybody in our company.

First, I have the accounting department print out a list of outstanding receivables. I then divide the past-due accounts among the various members of the executive staff. I take the most difficult accounts. We then call our equivalent staff person at the offending company to request payment.

For example, if I am in the role of CEO, then I call the CEO of the company that owes us money and indicate that there is a problem with getting paid. It is amazing what these calls can do because executives really *don't* like getting collection calls. They also smoke out any product or service problems that may be causing the holdup. I also have a policy of not paying commission on product that the customers have not paid for, which makes the salesperson a collection ally. I have been able to lower A/R days to 32 to 34 when terms are 30 days via this method.

With customers who are unable or unwilling to pay on time, I tend to take more drastic steps. These include:

- Developing payment terms on the customer's old invoices while paying for new product on a cash-in-advance basis

- Terminating the customer and resorting to legal collection methods including lawsuit or arbitration

Another method of mining receivables is to turn the very old ones (over 90 days) over to an internal employee who loves to collect old accounts, using an incentive of, say, 20 percent of what he or she collects and always being mindful of local laws and restrictions as to collection methods.

ACCOUNTS PAYABLE (A/P)

Another source of workable cash for a company can be accounts payable. By working payables to match receivables, one can often avoid the cash crunch that comes when there is a gap between the two. You can do this by negotiating payment terms with vendors based upon the time it takes to convert their items to finished goods and to receive payment from your customers. I have been able to negotiate terms in the 45- to 60-day range. An important feature of this negotiation is to pay on time so that you build credibility with your vendors.

Another way to make money from A/P is called the preemptive discount. This only works if you have available sources of cash at reasonable cost.

It works like this. Many companies offer discounts if you pay them within 10 days of receipt of goods; typically this discount is 1 or 2 percent of the bill. Now, suppose that you could pay a vendor immediately upon receipt of goods by wiring funds to it as soon as the goods were inspected for quality and quantity. What do you think the discount would be? I have been able to negotiate these preemptive discounts at values of 3 to 7 percent of the invoice price, depending on the vendor's need for cash. If one were to annualize this savings, what drops directly to bottom line is astronomical. Again, don't do this unless you have sufficient cash.

In the wholesale automotive-parts business there are institutionalized preemptive discounts of 12 percent if you pay in 30 days, decreasing 1 percent a month for 12 months until the discount is zero. This recognizes the often long-term nature of inventory in this business and incentivizes early payment.

INVENTORY

The fourth major asset element of the balance sheet is inventory. In managing inventory I always remember that all the mistakes and shortages of a corporation can be hidden in inventory. For example, if there is fraud or mismanagement, it usually ends up buried in the value of inventory. Overpurchasing or cost mistakes end up in inventory, and production overruns or mistakes end up in inventory.

The key in managing this element of the balance sheet is to realize that dead or overstated inventory creates problems, inasmuch as it reflects money tied up in a place where it cannot be used. Many companies are loath to write down or dispose of inventory because it will reduce earnings and may decrease the company's borrowing base. Because the turnaround manager's philosophy is to keep all assets at their true value so that he or she can decide the best way to manage those assets, I would encourage any reader to revalue his or her inventories at true value so he or she can take proper actions.

The best way to handle inventory is to identify those dead or slow-moving items and convert them into cash. There are several ways to do this:

- **Sell to nontraditional markets at deep discounts.** An example of this might be selling product into international markets where you currently don't sell. This way you don't disrupt traditional markets. You can often use experts in inventory disposal to assist you in this regard.

- **Use discount outlets.** The apparel industry has developed a healthy business for overruns through its factory outlets in discount malls. These outlets have been so successful that some companies now manufacture secondary, lower-quality lines specifically to sell through their discount stores. Some companies use TV shopping channels as outlets for overruns or slow-moving merchandise.

- **Rework inventory to convert it into usable and salable product.** This is purely an economic decision and relates to the cost of rework as opposed to sale at a discount.

- **Give inventory to charity or destroy it.** This is the last resort, but in some cases you can at least take a tax deduction.

Early in my career I was part of a large pharmaceutical company whose practice was to give its product overruns to charitable organizations for use worldwide. This was admirable from a humanitarian standpoint and assisted us in keeping our inventories at proper levels.

Until now I have primarily been discussing product in its finished state; however, I have not discussed those materials used in manufacture or in supporting office operations. The best way to keep raw materials at proper levels is never to order them in the first place. When I wrote my first book a number of years ago, the just-in-time inventory method (JIT) was a new concept. Briefly, JIT means that supplies arrive just prior to use so that a company gets and pays for product as it uses it and there is no cost associated with carrying raw materials. This concept is elegant and requires accurate planning and forecasting as well as suppliers who are impeccable in on-time delivery. In the real world, this seldom happens and for various reasons supplies arrive too soon or too late.

The auto industry has adopted JIT as a way of life and extracts huge fines from suppliers that miss their delivery times. In order to avoid these fines, suppliers have created safety stocks located near the manufacturing facilities. So in effect, the inventory point has moved down the supply chain and become part of the vendor's cost and responsibility. This form of JIT can reduce costs by, in essence, establishing supply points within a plant for vendors' products.

I recommend negotiating consignment arrangements with vendors in exchange for semiexclusive supply arrangements. This works in five steps:

1. Identify two or three major suppliers of materials that you currently use—items such as steel, boxes and

packing material, key components, and computer chips.

2. Indicate to the suppliers that they will be your key suppliers if they will stock items in your facilities in a bonded, fenced-off area; you will provide approximate numbers for your quarterly needs.

3. Take possession of the goods as they are removed from the bonded area, creating an invoice that you will pay under normal negotiated terms (30 to 60 days). The suppliers are free to inventory their products at any time.

4. Insure the product in your facilities.

5. Make it the suppliers' responsibility to ensure that an adequate supply of the product is present at all times.

What you have essentially done is create a JIT supply of product with minimal inventory costs.

One of the companies I ran used cobalt as a component of the final product. We had a small room full of over $5 million worth of cobalt. By taking the steps I described, I brought $5 million in cash back into the company by shortening my lead time from one month to zero and saved $250,000 in financing costs at a 5 percent annual borrowing rate.

I have successfully done this with computer chips, stainless steel, and a number of high-value components. I have done it with stationery supplies, packing materials, and print paper rolls for newspaper. In general, the supplier is pleased to be ensured of your business for a year while you are ensured of an instant supply and much lower working capital requirements.

I will discuss other balance sheet items such as reserves and loan balances in Chapters 10 and 17.

CHAPTER TEN

ANALYZING THE PROFIT AND LOSS STATEMENT

It's no surprise that a part of the process of increasing corporate profitability is a complete examination of the profit and loss statement (P&L) to determine what costs can be reduced or eliminated. However, a turnaround expert tends to look at things a different way. I have already discussed how to increase the revenues portion of the P&L by:

- Identifying strategic markets through the "slice and dice" analysis method

- Increasing margins on existing business through niche pricing

- Getting out of unprofitable market sectors and shedding unprofitable customers

Now the time has come to examine the rest of the P&L in regard to the expenses beyond cost of goods sold. These also reduce profitability and are often referred to as overhead. The examination of overhead items is equally important because all the gains made in the pricing and revenue-enhancement areas can be lost through unrealistic overhead structures. (I will discuss reducing cost of goods sold without compromising quality in Chapter 14.)

Let's examine each cost area below the gross margin line and utilize some of the turnaround secrets to provide cost reductions.

COMPENSATION

Compensation here usually refers to the pay of individuals not directly associated with making the product. It represents the pay of administrative and executive personnel. As I stated in Chapter 6, a green-field approach usually helps identify excess and/or needed positions in the organization. Only by running lean and trim can an organization keep this number under control.

BENEFITS

These are the individual benefits for employees, and they tie directly to compensation. They consist of:

- Health and dental insurance

- FICA

- Retirement plans

- Individual life insurance

- Vacation and sick pay

- Maternity pay

- Others

The mix of benefits and the percentage of gross compensation that they represent are determined by a combination of company desires, competitive hiring situations, and federal and state mandates. However, turnaround situations require that one judiciously look at these costs, which can reach 40 percent of base pay. The greatest and most rapidly escalating of these costs is most likely health and dental insurance. Costs for this item have increased 8 to 20 percent annually over the last decade and become very problematic when the inflation in other costs has been only 3 to 5 percent annually.

I believe that employees should participate in attempting to keep this cost item under control. This can be achieved by keeping employees informed of the problem, negotiating the best "deal" through your brokers each year, and sharing increases in costs with employees through increased deductibles, copays, and other financial incentives, which encourage employees to hold down discretionary medical visits. Another effective method of holding down costs is "opting out." It works like this: It costs approximately $1,000 to $1,600 per month to insure a family of four. If an employer picks up 80 percent of that cost, it is approximately $800 to $1,300 a month per employee. However, if an employee and her spouse both work and both have health plans at their places of employment, only one plan will pay benefits even though both plans are paid for. In this case I offer the employee an opportunity to "opt out" of my plan and will pay her an additional $400 a month to do so, thus saving $400 to $900 per month per employee. Employees must attest that other plans adequately cover them and must surrender their policies in writing. It is a "win–win" for the company and for the employee.

Another problem area for companies is the self-insured health plan in which companies pay claims on an "as incurred" basis through an administrator. This can be a cost-saving approach to medical insurance. Usually there is a blanket policy to cover a catastrophic event, and it has very high deductibles. But there is a real danger to the company when it eventually considers a sale or exit strategy, because in every self-insured plan there is a "tail" of unreported, unpaid claims that can harm the company. I do not recommend self-insurance as a general rule.

Another major area of benefit cost is the retirement plan, especially those to which there is a mandated corporate contribution. Many companies have been forced to declare bankruptcy in order to avoid the costs of such plans. In the 1990s there were many underfunded plans as a result of underperforming investments. Companies were required to "make up" the underfunding plus meet their continuing annual funding needs. These costs are called "legacy payments." Again, many companies declared Chapter 11 to avoid this oppressive burden. Right or wrong, this cost then shifted to the Pension Benefit Guarantee Corporation, a division of the federal government.

I usually attempt to move companies from mandated contributions to a voluntary contribution plan based on achievement of certain profit goals. This book isn't long enough to describe how this can be done, and a company needs legal experts to accomplish this. Companies can terminate old plans and put new, realistic ones into place.

Benefits, like other cost areas, are negotiable. They should reflect the nature of the business and what it can afford. But through judicious planning and negotiation, one can balance personal needs and cost.

INSURANCE

In this discussion, insurance refers to non–health insurance, such as property and casualty and product liability.

I once ran a company that had two refineries, each insured for $250 million with a maximum payout of $500 million if both were destroyed in the same year. The cost of such insurance was enormous, especially when one considered that the investors had paid only $20 million for each of the refineries, which were now old and somewhat decrepit. They were over 100 miles apart, so the probability of both being destroyed within a single year was infinitesimal. By setting realistic insurance needs, I was able to reduce premiums by hundreds of thousands of dollars.

I had another manufacturing company where the assets were

overinsured. I hired an insurance consultant to advise me about proper limits and deductibles. Since it was a multi-billion-dollar company, we saved over $1.2 million in annual premiums.

As a matter of procedure I always have an insurance consultant advise me on my current coverage plus ways to reduce premium costs without risk. Often it involves adding safety equipment or safety doors. Sometimes we find errors in classification of employee jobs, which directly affects workers compensation ratings. Thus, for the expenditure of $10,000 to $20,000 in consultant fees I save many times that amount in premiums.

FREIGHT

Most companies face the problem and cost of freight for both inbound materials and outbound finished product moving to customers. The cost of freight has continued to mount over the years as the cost of fuel has increased. It is not unusual today to find that your shipper is charging you a fuel surcharge for the recent escalation in their costs. But there are several things to remember in dealing with freight:

- All freight costs are negotiable.

- The more business you commit to one carrier, the greater the discount (as much as 60 percent).

- If you can ensure a carrier back-haul business, it can contribute to your savings. Back-haul simply means you can provide loads for your carrier in both directions.

- Freight charges are notoriously incorrect due to the arcane nature of the interstate tariff structure.

- Demurrage charges for taking excessive time to unload and load ships, rail cars, trucks, etc., can be almost as much as shipping costs.

■ The decision to own an internal fleet of trucks or to outsource this function is purely economic and service related and should not be colored by emotion.

I have found over recent years that companies would rather buy transportation services than own transportation services. Few companies are willing to build the infrastructure necessary to maintain, schedule, insure, and route a fleet of trucks unless there is a powerful economic incentive to do so. There are excellent competing services for shipping, which can assume this function on a worldwide basis including overnight services from the U.S. Postal Service, UPS, and FedEx.

A turnaround person will examine the structure of freight costs and will ask four key questions.

1. CAN FREIGHT COSTS BE PASSED BACK TO THE CUSTOMER?

To answer this, we examine our competitors. Either we calculate freight and deduct the cost from the price if we are offering free shipping in order to meet competitive practices, or we charge the customer freight plus handling costs. In other words, make freight a "cost recovery" or even a profit center.

I once was working on an offshore division of a company for which I was acting CEO. I noticed from the P&L that outbound freight costs seemed excessive. Upon investigation we discovered that the company offered a special program of free freight for orders over a certain size. The program was supposed to last for three months and then end. You guessed it! Three months came and went and the program became part of regular pricing. It was a year later when I started my investigation and discovered that we were spending $240,000 more a year in freight than we needed to. None of the competitors were matching the program, so it was easy to end.

2. CAN I RENEGOTIATE AND RESTRUCTURE
FREIGHT COSTS TO REDUCE THEM?

This involves a rebidding process with your carriers to determine what can be done to lower costs through mutual cooperation and placing a great majority of the business with one carrier. This process can be accomplished with the assistance of a freight consultant who will make recommendations to you on how to package product to reduce costs and how to determine the best mix of carriers and modes of transportation for your particular business (e.g., rail, truck, ship, air). In addition, a good freight consultant can help you negotiate more favorable rates.

I once operated a petroleum company that was shipping special crude oil from Utah to the East Coast of the United States. The freight consultant helped renegotiate with our existing carrier for better rates and tariffs. Meanwhile we made arrangements to process part of our crude in Utah. The combination saved us over $1 million in freight costs annually.

By redesigning packaging, especially for product imported from the Far East, we saved hundreds of thousands of dollars by packing more into the same cubic space.

3. ARE WE BEING CHARGED CORRECTLY
FOR THE SHIPPING WE ARE DOING?

Shipping companies often use the wrong tariff schedule in calculating shipping costs. There are companies that exist solely to check shipping bills and ensure that the billing is correct. They make their money by sharing the savings with their clients. The computer has diminished but not eliminated these errors, and hiring a freight checker is still a good idea.

4. AM I SPENDING NEEDLESSLY ON DEMURRAGE?

Demurrage is a charge for taking too long to get your products off the shipping vessel. In my first book, I describe a demurrage situation where we were remiss in promptly offloading ship tankers that were delivering crude oil to a Louisiana-based refinery. A simple change to the system allowed us to eliminate demurrage of $1,000 per day for the ships. Many companies forget that they have to pay up to $1,000 per day to delay offloading of railcars or trailer trucks. Making personnel aware of the problem often solves it. I have seen trailers sit for weeks as a convenient method of storage because no one focuses on the cost of keeping them.

A last area of concern is fraud. I have seen shipping clerks receive kickbacks in the form of rebates and gifts for directing shipping services to a favorite company. By taking control of the shipping function, the possibility of irregularities falls drastically.

TRAVEL AND ENTERTAINMENT

A necessary part of business is travel and entertainment, including corporate meetings, customer interaction, and conventions. The great dilemma is deciding when travel becomes unproductive and wasteful as opposed to useful and additive to corporate profits.

If I am entering a troubled company, or any company for that matter, I usually install a system of travel prejustification. In other words, I create an approval form that requires anyone who travels to identify the reason for the travel, what the trip is expected to yield from an economic standpoint, who is traveling, and for how long. The mere act of justifying travel will smoke out frivolous or ill-advised trips.

The cost of travel has increased over the years, especially to major cities and international locations. Yet there is no substitute for "pressing the flesh" and in-person analysis of situations. However, substitutes for in-person travel can be more extensive use of e-mail and teleconferencing. In a number of operations around the world I substituted video teleconferencing (which has become very inexpensive) for approximately half of our trips to Singapore, England, and France.

In addition to establishing travel-justification parameters, it is possible for any size company to establish discount deals with auto rental companies, hotel chains, and airlines. By controlling the travel choices, you can reduce travel costs up to 30 percent.

In addition to establishing rules for travel (e.g., everybody flies coach) you can limit airline costs. I normally establish a travel agent through whom we book all travel and who knows our "rules" for travel.

Unfortunately, the biggest "defeaters" of any travel policy are senior executives who feel that they are above the rules and circumvent them. For travel constraints to work, it should be understood that they are for everyone, from the CEO down!

A real conundrum is the "convention." Most industries have national or international conventions at which various competitors set up elaborate booths, ostensibly to market their products. I feel that because of the tremendous cost involved in attending these events, there need to be certain questions asked, or caveats established, prior to the decision to attend. These are:

- Does the convention allow you to take "orders" from the floor?

- Is convention attendance needed to show product to your distribution chain or potential new customers?

- Are the convention attendees the type of high-quality potential users of your goods or services whom you desire?

- Considering the cost, is it an efficient way to obtain new customers?

I have spent hundreds of thousands of dollars on conventions when I felt that the effort was worthwhile. Conversely I have pulled companies out of conventions that were unjustifiable from an economic standpoint.

The worst justification for attending a convention is to show the industry that you are still around. The advent of websites and the Internet has obviated the need to "show the flag" at a convention. If you feel compelled to show at a convention, at a minimum you should do the following six things:

1. Ensure that all convention meetings are scheduled in advance.

2. Set goals for the convention (e.g., sales volume, new distributors).

3. Set up dinner and lunch meetings in advance.

4. Set up sales meetings in conjunction with the convention.

5. Set up manning schedules for the booth—ensure that the right people are there at the right times.

6. After the convention, ensure that the salespeople follow up on leads and that they recap the results of the meeting (both good and bad) to determine if it was worthwhile.

In general, I don't have much use for most conventions but I recognize that they are an accepted part of life in some industries. I would rather take the money and time they take and apply these resources to one-on-one sales.

As I stated earlier, a good turnaround expert can cut travel and entertainment costs by 20–50 percent with essentially no effect on the company.

ENTERTAINMENT

Entertainment is one of the most difficult areas to control. It has also become expensive as a result of the IRS's position that only one half of the cost of business meals is deductible as an expense.

Thankfully the days of the two-martini lunch have disappeared into the mists of time; however, how does one control this area? The simplest answer is through limiting those who are authorized to entertain customers and then through a corporate understanding of what are acceptable levels of expense.

I have often insisted on reviewing all expense accounts in a company to determine if personnel are being prudent in their spending habits. I have often stated that I have never had an employee "pad" an expense account, because if I found out that she had attempted deceit, she would no longer be an employee.

As I stated in my first book, I have seen employees drink themselves into stupors and ruin their health over the long term all in the name of entertainment. Common sense is the key here—and it is difficult to legislate common sense.

LEASES AND RENTAL COSTS

In bankruptcy one is allowed to "reject" executory contracts. Leases are considered executory contracts, and the shedding of unwanted lease and rental arrangements is a great advantage of Chapter 11 proceedings. In the absence of taking this extreme action, one is forced to negotiate with landlords. Turnaround experts regularly renegotiate leases.

In Chapter 8 I discussed how to build a back door into leases during negotiation. Unfortunately most companies haven't provided such an escape hatch, so renegotiation is called for.

The first step in lowering rentals and leases is to understand your position. A study to determine if the rents you are paying are competitive is mandatory prior to beginning your efforts. For example, one company I worked with had leased but never occupied office space in Manhattan. The space was costing $100,000 per month but the company had experienced hard times prior to moving to the facilities and had even purchased and installed expensive new furniture in the office space.

The landlord was adamant that we continue to honor a lease that had four years left to run. No amount of negotiation seemed to work until we found a technical problem with the lease. We finally settled for three months' rent and leaving the furniture behind in order to get out of the obligation.

On other occasions I have been able to renegotiate leases based on over-market rates or certain nonperformance by the landlord. For example, in one retail chain we identified properties where the company was losing money and restructured the rent from a fixed payment to a percentage of our cash flow.

Some other negotiating tools one can use include:

■ Extending the lease for financial consideration now

■ Changing the basis for the lease

■ Swapping locations for another one that the landlord owns

Most companies shy away from renegotiating because of the mere existence of the lease document. I feel that most landlords are reasonable businesspeople who wish to keep a tenant and wish to see them succeed. In *almost every* renegotiation effort I have been able to achieve some savings. One must merely have the chutzpah (nerve) to start the renegotiation process.

LEGAL COSTS

Depending on the type of business you are in, legal costs can be quite significant. These costs break down into three areas:

1. Patent and other intellectual property costs

2. Normal contractual obligations, including acquisition costs

3. Lawsuits

Unless they are extremely large or have need for internal legal function due to the number of matters handled as part of the regular business, most companies outsource their legal help.

One of the most helpful resources can be your attorney. Conversely, a poor attorney can be an impediment to growth and a deal breaker, not a deal maker. The key is to identify counsel, both internal and external, who has good business sense but also has a balanced approach to business risk. These people are identified through their reputations and recommendations of others.

A good patent attorney can help you build a portfolio of intellectual property, including trademarks and brands that can carry extremely large values in the event of a sale. For example, I know of companies that have utilized licensing of brand names and patents as major sources of income. Many companies are reticent to spend the money on this endeavor, but in most instances it is well worthwhile to protect what you have developed.

In the area of contracts and acquisitions, a good attorney can help you avoid problems in the future through intelligent crafting of documents.

Needless to say, the ultimate and least satisfying use of attorneys is lawsuits. Unfortunately we live in a litigious world and you will be forced to defend yourself or sue many times during your business career. The key to winning any lawsuit is to hire the best attorney you can find who can advise you on the merits of your case as well as the economics of the lawsuit. Remember that litigation is a process into which one goes in as a pig and emerges as a sausage.

One of the worst days in my business career was realizing that I might have to sue my own attorney for overbilling. A company that I had as a client was suing another company for fraudulent conveyance in an acquisition. The company we were suing had grossly overstated its backlogs of orders and projections of future sales. Our attorney, who was already deep into the case when I was hired, had indicated that an early resolution would occur.

Despite my pleadings for detailed billings and economic estimates of cost to pursue the legal action, the attorney wasn't responding. The case dragged on and a bill from the attorney finally showed up. The bill was for several million dollars. Obviously, I was aghast at the amount and called for a legal audit by an independent firm that specializes in such things.

It turned out that our case had become a "dumping ground" for hourly charges by everyone in the firm. We were paying $200 per hour for secretaries to copy documents and many other overcharges. After threatening to sue, we settled the case and our attorney's fees, and we avoided a potential disaster.

In evaluating legal costs, one should get estimates of the costs of any action well in advance of the activity. A real signal as to the merits of the case is to ask the attorney if she will take it on contingency, or as percentage of the award. If it is a strong case, most attorneys will consider a contingency arrangement.

In any case, keeping current on legal costs and their potential result is very important. In staff meetings, I always ask for a review of legal items, including costs, and this review should be part of board of directors meetings.

ADVERTISING, INCLUDING THE INTERNET

I was involved with a retail chain that had used full-page newspaper ads very effectively; however, the company's advertising costs as a percentage of sales were twice as great as its nearest competition's. We began to decrease the ad frequency slowly to determine at which point sales volume would begin to suffer. We found that at frequency levels above 110 percent of that of the competition there was no appreciable change in sales. Thus, we had reached consumer saturation at the 110 percent level, and any spending above that level was wasted.

Advertising and promotion are obviously your ways of reaching the consumer. I find it interesting that in troubled times, when sales are not doing well, companies will cut back on their advertising budgets to save money but will spend more on advertising during the good times. *This is counterintuitive.* Under adverse conditions, companies should spend more in order to capture a greater share of a diminishing market.

The secret of advertising is effectiveness. This combines ad design, the type of media, the frequency, and the follow-through system. A good advertising agency can advise you about the proper combination of these elements, and a good public relations firm can get media attention at lower costs than a full-blown ad campaign.

In industrial environments where you are selling products to other businesses, a combination of direct mail and ads in industry-related magazines is the proper approach, whereas consumer products may require a combination of print, radio, and TV advertising.

Ways to save on advertising yet continue to get your message out there include:

- Using black-and-white instead of color ads.

- Swapping product or services for advertising. Radio stations do this often and I have swapped product for print space in newspapers. I once ran an outdoor sign company that regularly swapped excess billboard space for things such as restaurant meals and office supplies.

- Never printing prices on brochures—this keeps the brochures usable even if you change pricing.

- Testing the effectiveness of print ads on radio and TV spots by offering a discount if the consumer mentions the ad or brings in a coupon.

Almost every company today needs a good website. Consumers have learned to preshop on the Internet and are better informed prior to making a purchasing decision than ever before. It is important that you obtain the proper links to your site on search engines so that your product or service appears among early choices when people put certain key words into a search engine.

This service is performed by Internet marketing specialists, and I encourage the use of such individuals. Also, the website should capture information from a potential buyer if the buyer so desires; that is, the website should make it easy for a potential buyer to contact the company or order product.

Your website should tell your story and be a selling tool; thus, if it is to remain fresh, it should be modified at least every six months, or more often if possible. A website is a living interactive reflection of the company and can do harm if it becomes stale.

The sum of all this is that advertising should be appropriate to your business model and doesn't necessarily have to cost an arm and a leg. The information you received from benchmarking can give you clues as to what competitors spend and how they spend it. Again, the key to advertising is utilizing a really good ad agency that can guide you in the selection of both media and the type of ads that are proper for your business and fit your budget needs.

TELEPHONE, FAX, AND E-MAIL

Unfortunately, with the advent of new and broader methods of communication, the opportunities for abuse have also expanded. I don't mean to sound overly controlling, but you need to control the use of telephone, fax, and e-mail in order to ensure that these resources are not being wasted.

Let's review the various forms of communication. They are:

- Telephone (both cellular and landline)
- Fax
- E-mail, including text messaging
- Teleconferencing
- U.S. Postal Service (snail mail)
- Courier services (including the U.S. Postal Service)

Just like any other vendor, you need to evaluate telephone services on a regular basis. Due to the highly competitive nature of the telephone and all phone business, the costs of this form of communication have dropped over the years. However, some companies have locked themselves into contracts for service and equipment that are well above market. It is important to examine these systems and negotiate new deals that can save significant amounts of money over the long term. There are also new options such as voice over internet protocol (VOIP), which are emerging as low-cost alternatives to standard long-distance service.

Moreover, most new computer-based phone systems can control access and control who can make long-distance or international calls. Most phone systems have the ability to print out phone records on a continuous basis. The mere mention of this record keeping and the desire that employees eliminate or limit personal calls can reduce long-distance calling *by 50 percent.*

It's not only the cost of the calls but rather the inefficiency that such abuse causes that is the most disturbing. I have detected people calling phone sex numbers and relatives abroad until I took the precautionary steps.

E-mail abuses are also a major problem. I find that people will e-mail associates sitting in the office space next to them rather than getting up and speaking to them. Companies need to make personnel aware that e-mails are not for casual conversation and can, and often are, used as evidence in court. I have acted as an expert witness in a number of court cases, and part of the incriminating evidence has been e-mails among the parties. The parties never expected the e-mails to be published in a court of law. Also there is the problem of explicit or pornographic websites, for which an employer may find itself liable in a sexual harassment lawsuit.

There are programs that monitor computer activity. Employees should be advised that such programs are being used and the consequences of improper action. By taking these few simple steps, you can reduce the cost of communication dramatically.

As far as mail and courier services are concerned, by establishing adequate approvals for their use and tracking these costs separately, one can gain control of these expenses.

Earlier in this chapter I discussed the use of teleconferencing in place of travel. I believe it is a great cost-saving tool. There are now a number of low-cost, dial-in teleconferencing services that can be utilized. The company should identify the service to be used and who within the organization is authorized to set up teleconferences so that this area of communication is not abused. Fax facilities should be treated in the same manner as telephone communication and may even be centralized.

A great many of the cost-saving solutions I have provided to this point sound like micromanagement and for that I apologize, but I have seen and lived through so many inefficiencies and abuses that I would be remiss if I didn't learn from these painful lessons.

ENERGY COSTS (FUEL, NATURAL GAS, POWER, ETC.)

Energy costs represent an ever-growing problem for most companies. As I write this, the cost of oil has risen to over $70 per barrel, and the cost of energy has affected companies with regard to the power and gas that they consume, the fuel that they use for shipping, and the energy used in their supplies and in the petrochemicals and petrochemical-based supplies that they utilize. All companies use energy to a greater or lesser extent. The question is how to reduce the cost of this very valuable consumable.

FUEL

This is gasoline or diesel for your cars or trucks. Companies have tried to reduce this cost by signing long-term contracts with certain suppliers, but in the long run this has a minimal effect in the form of small discounts.

The real answer is to switch to cheaper fuel and fuel blends as well as engines that can burn biofuels such as ethanol. There is an economic trade-off of revamping versus continuing with normal gasoline engines. The cost may not be worth it in the short run.

NATURAL GAS

I have been successful in saving natural gas by purchasing in the summer when the cost is low and storing the gas for my year-round needs. Your gas usage needs to be significant, but savings of 20 percent are possible by doing this. This also assumes that the company has the available cash to purchase gas in advance.

POWER

Power is something everyone can save. Every company uses power: power for manufacturing, power for air-conditioning, power for lighting.

Power in a business environment can be separated into two components for billing purposes: consumption and peak demand. Consumption is exactly what it sounds like. It is the volume of power used over some period of time, usually expressed as kilowatt hours (kWh). The second component is peak demand, that is, the maximum rate at which a company draws power in any day. The peak demand is of special concern to power companies because they must construct facilities to cover peaks as well as normal demand. It is because of peak loads (such as air-conditioning loads in the summer) that there are brownouts.

To cover their costs, the power companies set their rate schedules based on maximum demand within a very short time period. The volume under the demand-rate schedule then determines what a company is charged. Thus, a company sets its rate schedule by starting up multiple pieces of machinery, which draw a great deal of power initially, or by starting up several air-conditioning units at the same time.

The secret that most companies don't realize is to stagger start-ups to reduce peak demand. For example, I was once called in to help a company that used electric sintering furnaces to make tiny metal balls for use in fabricating prelubricated bearings. It had four large furnaces and started them all up at the same time in the morning. The furnaces drew tremendous amounts of power as they overcame the initial resistance of starting up, causing a gigantic peak demand. By staggering start-ups by 15 minutes, we changed our peak demand characteristics and shifted the company onto a lower rate schedule that saved over $500,000 a year.

One of the hottest selling devices on the market for industrial applications these days is a peak-demand computer that attaches to your main power line and allows you to set peak demand limits. It prevents you from bringing on too much electricity too quickly. Your power provider can help find and install this type of equipment.

Another way to save energy costs is to elect to use interruptible power. This means that the electric company can reduce the power provided to your company on "x" hours' notice in order to balance loading. Although some utilities don't offer this option, many do. If you can stand a temporary reduction in power, this option usually carries the lowest rate schedule available.

There are also commonsense alternatives such as power-management computers that automatically shut down lights and other power-using equipment at preset times in a 24-hour period. Teaching personnel to conserve electricity can also save on power consumption.

Your power utility and gas companies will conduct free conservation surveys to teach you how to save on electricity, gas, or heating oil. Also one can see that utility rates and bills can be quite confusing. Just as there are companies that review freight bills, there are companies that review utility bills for errors and share the savings with you. These companies earn a percentage (usually 50 percent) of the savings they generate purely by auditing the bills. If they want to charge up-front fees for their efforts, don't use them.

WARRANTY EXPENSE

Warranties can be considered a major opportunity, a sales expense, or a cost center. Let me explain. I once ran a company that made thermally insulated glass windows and had developed a new process for fabricating and sealing the windows. In view of its new process, it decided to offer a three-year warranty on the new windows as opposed to a normal six-month warranty. In addition, it agreed in its advertising to take windows back "for any failure." The program worked as an advertising ploy and sales increased 10 percent; however, warranty replacement began to soar. The company had made a nearly fatal error: It had failed to understand the nature of its customers—building contractors who tend to handle building supplies somewhat roughly and consider normal breakage of windows as a cost of construction.

This cost was now passable back to my client, the manufacturer, which began facing enormous warranty costs. The warranty had been poorly written and my client had failed to realize the consequences of its actions.

In another instance, I was able to improve the warranty on a new high-tech thermal printer we were about to market, but only after extensive testing and determination that there would be no appreciable increase in warranty costs. We also obtained backup warranties from various high-wear component manufacturers. In other words, we really gave away nothing in order to get a very positive marketing tool.

Another approach is to use warranties as a profit center. Most major appliance manufacturers and auto dealers offer extended warranties on their products. These extended warranties are very, very profitable and the revenue stream from such programs can exceed the profit from the original product sale. The reason for this is that most manufacturers have lowered the "infant mortality rate" on their products and know almost exactly when units will begin to fail. By knowing this fact, they can adjust the stream of charges for extended warranties to generate strong cash flow. They can exclude or charge more for high-wear parts that they know will fail early. They can also exclude "abuse" of the product as a condition of the warranty claim.

Retailers typically pass warranty claims back to the manufacturers with impunity and usually have agreements that allow them to do so. But a major weakness in many companies is the methodology they utilize for handling warranty and repair claims. There are unscrupulous people out there who take advantage of companies with regard to claims. The answer to this is a method of tracking and classifying repairs and replacements and keeping the customer informed via e-mail each step of the way. By doing this you can inform the customer of any charges for items not within warranty parameters and obtain approval for any noncovered expenses.

In the same way extended warranties can be used as a profit center, factory repairs can also be used as a method of generating positive income and profit streams. There are also companies that will perform this service for you on a nationwide or worldwide basis and will provide on-site repairs for the customer. This is a good solution for companies that do not wish to devote internal resources to this effort. The arrangement with these outside repair companies will often involve selling parts to them at a discount, plus some sharing of repair revenue.

In summary, the keys to keeping warranty costs low are to:

- Match the warranty to competitive conditions, your product or service, and the nature of the market.

- Get a good attorney to write your warranty so that it is not overly onerous and provides for the proper conditions for exercise of the claim.

- Use extended warranties as a profit center or as a selling tool.

- Monitor and track product warranty or service warranties, and keep the customer informed of status or any extra charges.

- Monitor and track repairs and utilize this function as a profit center.

SUPPLIES

Did you ever notice that right around Christmas or at the beginning of school in the fall, supplies and paper goods are being consumed more rapidly? Or if you look in desk drawers, you and others have a "stash" of pens, paper, and other supplies? For fear of sounding petty, I'm not going to spend long on this expense item, but it is a cost and most companies don't focus on this cost of doing business. By merely having a supply closet or room and having one individual dispense and order supplies on an "as needed" basis, this expense can be reduced significantly. It's up to you if you wish to have a department charge-back system for this item, but it's a method of controlling one of those expenses that often gets lost in the overall scheme of things. In service businesses or advertising agencies the cost of offices supplies can be quite large.

Another area of supplies that can be very sizable is factory consumables. Items in this category are things like lubricants, grinding wheels, tools, and safety gear such as helmets and safety glasses. These often get lumped into the cost of goods sold category.

The larger the company, the bigger the amount spent on factory consumables. In one company, I found that the white cotton gloves we provided to personnel for polishing chromed parts were disappearing at an alarming rate. A brief investigation provided us with the alarming knowledge that we were unknowingly providing communion gloves to most of the town of Rockford, Illinois. By making the gloves yellow and imprinting them with the company name, the shrinkage slowed to normal levels. In another company, I found massive kickbacks by merely tracking the inflation on our usage of consumable products. In one company, our sales had not grown for several years but our consumables costs were growing at 10–15 percent per year. One of our more sea-soned purchasing agents was perpetrating the fraud. The kickbacks were over $1 million a year. Needless to say, we had an early termination and pressed for a criminal conviction. I will discuss fraud in more detail in Chapter 18.

TAXES

One of the biggest expenses in business, taxes, is considered last in the list of controllable expenses. Considering that the tax man can take 50 percent or more of your profits in federal, state, and local taxes, one needs to be very aggressive in approaching this cost item. There is an absolute need for a very good tax consultant. A tax consultant can alert you to legal opportunities to reduce tax costs on a continuing basis. This gold–plated individual may or may not be part of your auditing firm and is usually found by word of mouth. The various tax laws always confuse me because they are continually changing, and despite protestations to the contrary they seem to become more and more confusing and ar-cane.

If you plan well in advance, you can legally minimize your exposure to the bite of the tax man (or woman). Some instances of this approach that I have used are:

- Establishment of a Section 931 corporation in Puerto Rico for the construction of facilities and the creation of new jobs in that country. The added profits paid for a new production facility within seven months.

- Donation of underutilized facilities and land to the local community in exchange for write-offs.

- Use of maximum legal depreciation to reduce profit and taxes.

- Use of research and development write-offs to match cost with revenues.

- Use of capital gains deductions where appropriate in the sale of facilities.

- Use of tax-free swaps of facilities.

Now, one must remember that many of the tax-reduction methods I may utilize also reduce taxable profits. This may cause duress in public companies or companies that are being prepared for sale.

An example of this was a privately held outdoor-sign company, referred to in Chapter 1. The company would spend approximately $30,000 to $60,000 (at that time) on the construction of new signs. The tax code allowed us to depreciate these signs over five years. The average life of a sign was 30 years. We were growing rapidly and were keeping our profits at a minimum through this perfectly legal device. Our cash flow was very large, but our P&L did not reflect this due to the high depreciation expense. Our local banker called to discuss the company's mediocre financial statements and the fact that standard performance ratios were showing us to be a less-than-desirable client. Despite my explanation of what we were doing to reduce taxes, the banker was unsympathetic and wanted to terminate the relationship. My ire was raised to the boiling point and I called the president of the bank to explain our situation to a rational person.

Fortunately he "got it" and I never saw the hapless soul who delivered the bad news again. We eventually sold the company and the price was based on a multiple of the company's earnings before interest, taxes, depreciation, and amortization. Since this calculation reflected our cash flow, we were in great shape.

As you can see, it is desirable to reduce taxable income without reducing cash flow. The law also allows the use of legitimate reserves for things such as litigation, bad debt, and inventory shrinkage as proper reductions in profits. You should take guidance from your tax consultant on these items as well.

There are many businesses that have special tax considerations such as depletion, which refers to the use of mineral or oil assets, for example. Your tax consultant should have knowledge of the special tax provisions that are applicable to your specific business.

Another time that a really good tax person can help immensely is when you are preparing for sale. There are tax–minimization approaches that can help a seller or purchaser, and you should have full knowledge of them prior to the transaction. The caveat I place upon this consideration is not to let the tax considerations drive the deal, but use them as one factor in your consideration.

CHAPTER ELEVEN

SYSTEMS/THE COMPUTER/ THE INTERNET

I was once on the board of a company that had installed an integrated "enterprise" system. It was supposed to integrate all the various elements of the business into one smooth-flowing, highly visible model of efficiency. It contained everything from customer-tracking data to order entry to production planning. It was supposed to help with component orders and purchasing. It was supposedly able to plan shipping and generate all the associated accounting and management reports. The software plus attendant installation and consulting costs were over $30 million. This did not include the cost of hardware or internal personnel salaries.

Our top season (Christmas) came and the CEO informed the board that we couldn't ship because of computer problems.

There are numerous times that this story has been repeated, where instead of being a tool, the computer has become a major, very expensive impediment to the business.

Now, don't get the idea that I am anticomputer. I think that every business today can utilize this powerful tool. To suggest that a company operate without some degree of computer assistance is like suggesting that we do away with telephones or automobiles. But in the company I mentioned, we ended up dismantling the system and replacing it. It harmed the company greatly, not to mention the time lost on the resultant lawsuits. Most of the deeply troubled companies I was engaged to help had usually just purchased new computer systems and expanded their warehouse facilities.

There are a number of questions a company must ask itself when it prepares to identify a system for its needs. (Note that I use the word *system,* not *computer,* because the computer is the box and the system is what it does. Let's take each question in turn.

1. WHAT DO I WANT MY SYSTEM TO DO?

Identifying business needs requires thought. The primary thing to do in this exercise is to start with a blank sheet of paper and identify the most pressing informational needs of your business.

For example:

- Customer identification and tracking

- Order entry and tracking

- Product inventory and location

- Shipping and billing

- Receivables

On a second sheet of paper you should identify the "would like to have" items such as:

- Customer-warranty claims tracking

- Tracking of factory consumables

- Online order status

It's like buying a car. In the car-buying process you mentally identify your must-haves first, such as reliability, seat six comfortably, and space for cargo, and "would like" items such as color, leather seats, a CD player, and heated seats.

You should review these lists with your personnel in order to refine them. Each person should color the list with his or her own wants and perceived requirements, but it is up to you to sort through the final lists to determine what the final must-haves are. For example, your information technology (IT) person will want the latest and greatest computer system available. You must then measure the benefits of all these requests and needs against their costs.

One should remember that in dealing with computer systems, the major cost today is not the equipment that you purchase but rather the software, its support, and the internal and external maintenance of the systems, including security and backups.

2. HOW CAN THE SYSTEM MAKE MY BUSINESS MORE EFFICIENT, COMPETITIVE, AND PROFITABLE?

For example, a customer-tracking list could allow you to retain 10 to 20 percent more of your first-time customers. An order-entry system might reduce lost orders by 15 percent and add to customer retention. An inventory-tracking system would reduce shrinkage and lost orders. The same analysis should be applied to the "would like" lists.

3. WHAT WILL BE THE COST/BENEFIT OF ANY SYSTEM THAT I INSTALL?

You are now prepared to assign approximate costs to each of these options and begin to understand the cost/benefit of everything you choose.

A good IT person can help you sort through the maze of equipment and computer software available today. Smaller companies should strive to utilize off-the-shelf, less expensive hardware and software in order to minimize costs. But in the cost/benefit analysis, you may find that the cost of some systems may not be justified by the benefits they might bring, and as a result you may wish to seek alternatives, including manual systems that might meet your needs.

I once became CEO of a company that was installing a large, very complex accounting and manufacturing system that was much too large for the company. The cash flow was killing us. I found that the chief financial officer had become enamored with the software at his old company (which was much larger) and was determined to install the same system in my much smaller operation.

Having determined that it was totally inappropriate to our needs, I terminated work on the program and asked the CFO to leave our employ. Three years later I was called in to assist a very small high-tech manufacturer of satellite ground stations and found that the CFO was the same individual I had fired. He was attempting to install the same costly and sophisticated computer system at his new employer. He resigned without a word from me. This little example illustrates why the initial needs-planning process is so important to the overall development of a computer strategy that is right for your company.

4. WHAT INTERNAL RESOURCES WILL I NEED (PEOPLE, MONEY, FACILITIES, EQUIPMENT)?

The fourth question addresses the ongoing permanent resources companies need to keep any system going. This is a cost of doing business and must be considered when designing or purchasing a computer system. Companies will decide that they need to design systems for their own particular needs and are shocked when they realize that there are enormous continuing costs associated with documenting, updating, and training on these custom systems.

These are costs you must consider when you are calculating

the cost/benefit of applications that you would like for your new system. These costs decrease as you move toward standardized systems or off-the-shelf systems that are modified slightly to meet your individual company needs.

5. WILL THERE BE A DISRUPTION IN MY OPERATIONS AS A RESULT OF CHANGING SYSTEMS? CAN I MAKE IT SEAMLESS?

These are major concerns. The good news is that if an installation is planned and phased in properly, there need be only a minimal disturbance, if any, to the current operations. The key is the timing of how new systems are implemented. Operate your current and new systems in parallel until the new system "proves" its ability to operate properly.

6. WHAT PERIPHERAL SYSTEMS WILL I NEED?

In calculating the cost of systems, one must also consider the cost and investment in workstations, printers, carriers, and other input devices such as bar-code scanners and printers or radio frequency identification devices (RFIDs). In restaurants, the cash register has become an input device and even the bar guns that pour the beverages can provide automatic inputs to a system. In a large facility, the cost of these input and output devices can mount quickly as well as the cost of interconnecting all of these devices to your computing stations.

7. HOW LONG IS WHAT I AM PLANNING TO DO VIABLE, AND CAN I SCALE IT WITH MY BUSINESS?

The real question is, Can the system be modified so that it can be used in the future? Computers, both software and hardware, can become obsolete technologically in a one- to three-year time frame, and you want to know your alternatives in the event of early obsolescence. In addition, you want to know if you can easily expand your system to meet the future needs of the company at reasonable costs.

TIPS FOR INSTALLATION AND IMPLEMENTATION

Now you are ready to look for the proper software and hardware to meet your corporate needs. Here are ten important tips:

1. Fit the computer and software to meet your corporate size and growth rate.

2. Identify and cost your must-haves in a computer system down to the types of reports you wish to have.

3. Measure the cost/benefit relationship of the software and hardware you plan to purchase and eliminate those areas that do not provide clear economic rationales for their purchase.

4. Ensure that any system (software) that you install is modular—that is, that the failure of one subsystem does not bring down the functionality of all others. Failure to do this is like having an automobile that can't run if a taillight is out.

5. Evaluate your peripheral input and output devices to ensure that you are utilizing the optimum methods of getting data into the computer and reports out. I once ran a company that manufactured bar-code printing devices and we weren't using bar coding in our own operations. The installation of bar coding helped drop product lead times by one week and inventories by 50 percent.

6. Ensure that your software and hardware companies are reliable and warranty their work. In the case of the

company that couldn't ship at Christmas, the software supplier did a great deal of finger-pointing at us and the subcontractors they recommended we hire.

7. Develop hard schedules for installation of hardware and software with your suppliers and penalties for not meeting performance or timing guarantees.

8. Ensure that you operate systems in parallel before going "live" on the new system.

9. Develop a disaster-recovery plan in advance so that if or when a problem occurs, you have a fallback method of salvaging the business.

10. Make sure that your IT manager is up to the task—if he or she is not, get someone who is!

If I sound paranoid about this whole computer area, it's because I am! I have spent many sleepless nights worrying about the abilities of both internal and external personnel to deliver on computer and software promises. I have worked people night and day to meet deadlines and both fired and promoted people based on performance.

The funniest story with regard to a computer system relates to the installation of a totally "new" system for a pharmaceutical manufacturer that had multiple plants in various cities. We were going from a very basic, very limited, obsolete information system to a system that would give us real-time operations reports. In this process, I identified a young IT manager who was brilliant and extremely motivated in leading one portion of the project. The headquarters and nerve center for our efforts was to be a facility in eastern Pennsylvania in a relatively small town. This young genius lived in New York City and commuted to work (which we paid for). His hours were quite erratic and he came to work in the middle of the night or often would work several days in a row without a break. Because he was performing well, I had no problem with this. One day he came to ask if he could move "here."

I thought he meant the small town and was surprised because he was a bachelor—a move to the town might reduce his limited social life to zero—so I asked him why he wanted to move to town.

He said I had misinterpreted what he was asking. He wanted to move to the plant for the duration of the project and asked that we install a bed in the computer room. I compromised and got a trailer for him and put him in the plant parking lot, which he called home for the next two years.

Needless to say, he was priceless.

Even though this story isn't totally applicable, it's fun and it's true, and it illustrates the kind of flexibility one needs in various situations.

SALES

A major portion of most companies' cost structure is the effort devoted to sales. When I write about sales, I do so with great trepidation because I have found that almost every company I have helped has utilized a different combination of techniques and personnel to drive sales. It is also the area where I have achieved the greatest success and the worst disappointments. I have been lied to, cajoled, stroked, and assured by sales managers. I have developed great sales organizations and have had the greatest difficulty in molding a team.

The reason for all of this uncertainty is the fact that salespeople and sales managers by their very nature are optimists and as such tend to overestimate their ability to deliver sales. In addition, the sales performance of a company may be influenced by external conditions such as economic fluctuations or changing market-sector conditions. Competitive actions also influence their ability to sell.

Now, many of you may disagree with what I am about to write, but it is derived from many painful lessons: The *only* thing that counts in marketing and sales is the ability to deliver promised numbers.

The really successful corporate leaders I know are unmerciful in driving the sales organization to achieve mutually agreed-upon goals. This is not to say that marketing and sales techniques can't be modified to assist the sales effort, but presuming the goals were set with the assistance of the sales department, excuses and alibis don't cut it with me anymore and I begin to seek new personnel when objectives are not achieved.

If your sales are not what they should be, there may be several causes:

1. You are not telling your story properly.

2. You are not selling through the proper channels.

3. Your sales department is not exercising the proper effort.

4. There is a problem with the product or service you are selling.

Let's examine each of these efforts in turn.

1. YOU ARE NOT TELLING THE STORY PROPERLY

The years and numerous rejections have taught me that 50–75 percent of a successful sales effort depends on a formalized discussion of the competitive advantages of the product or service you offer. Developing a coherent "story" that you can tell the prospective client shows professionalism and avoids the mistake of omitting big advantages that you can offer the client. You can integrate this story into a verbal presentation, a PowerPoint presentation, a brochure, a website, flip charts, and numerous other presentation methods.

Formal presentations are especially important when providing technical comparisons with competitive products. Let me describe a real-life example where the presentation made all the difference.

I had a client who was in the business of providing packaged candy and cheeses as a method of fund-raising for high school and college football teams and bands. The methodology was as follows: The school's athletic director or band director would select a provider of a food or candy package. The provider (my client) would then provide brochures to the students so that these packages could be sold in a fund-raising program. These sales would be to friends and family. The students would collect orders and money and turn them over to the provider. The provider would then deliver the specified packages to the school for distribution by the students and would split any profits with the school 50/50.

My client had been in business for 20 years and had been quite successful in its efforts. It had a warehouse and used seasonal labor (military spouses) for its programs, which occurred mainly in the spring and fall at the beginning of school sessions. Everything was going along swimmingly until some "moms and pops" decided to go into the business, offering limited services but modifying the split of profits to 60 percent for the school and 40 percent to the provider. This 10 percent swing would have driven my client into a break-even or a loss position if he were to match their pricing structure.

I began questioning him about the advantages and disadvantages of his business versus the others. First of all we determined that the customer was the band or athletic director and that these people tended to be conservative in their thinking and risk taking in most decisions. In other words, if they were to select a provider and program, their objectives were clearly to select a program that:

- Was approved by the parent-teacher association and school administration

- Delivered the desired outcome (sufficient funds for their program)

- Was safe (we were selling food products)

I now asked my client about his selling technique. He stated that he would go through his brochure verbally with the potential buyer and describe the financial arrangements, hoping to get the business.

I asked my client whether, in view of the conservative nature of his customer, he had ever had a failure to deliver. He stated that once and only once in his time in business, due to a late delivery of food, he was unable to provide product in a timely manner, and as a result the program did not deliver the expected profits. He then "made up" the difference to the school. I leapt upon this disclosure, stating that he had offered a warranty even though it was only once. I also asked if he had insurance in case anyone got sick from the food products. He stated that even though the food companies stood behind their products, he carried an additional $5 million in liability insurance (which the moms and pops did not). I finally asked if any of his customers ever visited his facilities and saw the substance and capital invested in his business. The answer was no!

We then decided to modify our marketing program to reflect our advantages and play upon the concerns of his customers. We decided that a set of flip charts was the way to make our presentation. There were four charts.

The first chart was a huge blowup of a gold-edged document that was titled "Warranty." It offered the customers an assured payout on their programs. In addition, the salesperson would carry a pad of warranty documents that he or she would fill in for the specific situation. Because the company controlled the warranty amount and had a negative event only once, it represented a low-risk sales tool that the small operators would be loath to match.

The second chart was an enlarged version of the client's $5 million insurance policy, which assured the customer that no matter what occurred, the purchaser was adequately covered. Of course, small operators could not match this cost.

The third chart contained photos of the plant and facilities to show that a company of substance stood behind the program.

The fourth chart contained the brochure to show the selection of products available.

In addition to all this, I asked the owner to raise his prices 10 percent with the understanding that the 10 percent increase would partially offset the differential in split.

The idea really worked! Within one year, most of the "moms and pops" were out of business because they could not compete with the concept that my client was selling. Yet we had not changed anything except how we presented those advantages that we already possessed.

In a retail environment the "story" must be told through advertising and the physical appearance of the retail establishment. It must say that you are a discount store or a high-end, high-quality location. In the instance of the jewelry chain in Chapter 5, it had achieved almost perfect market segmentation through three types of stores.

The first was a branded small operation designed for the youth market. It carried lower-priced trendy jewelry that was affordable to the 16- to 25-year-old purchaser who was very style conscious. The quality of the jewelry was very good. The store was designed to appeal to a very young crowd and used very slick displays, with its advertising carrying the same theme.

The second level was designed to appeal to upscale 25- to 50-year-olds; it included very fine watches and designer jewelry with prices suitable for an affluent and upwardly mobile client. Again, the story was completed through advertising that appealed to this type of customer.

The third brand was for senior, more mature customers and had its own store design. It carried jewelry and gift items and emphasized service. The trio of businesses recognized the needs of each of its types of consumers precisely and covered the potential market.

The point of all this is to recognize your story and use it to market to your potential client base. If your story doesn't work, change it! And don't be afraid to modify it or fine-tune it. Turnaround people are very adept at recognizing when a story is no longer effective and are prepared to develop a new one that works.

2. YOU ARE NOT SELLING THROUGH
THE PROPER CHANNELS

I once ran a company that was dedicated to selling its products through distributors exclusively while its competitors utilized multiple channels such as direct sales and Internet sales. We were complimented for sticking to a "price" model and for being true to our distribution partners. It was a mistake because our competitors grew at a faster rate than we did and generated greater profit per sale.

As the end user becomes more and more sophisticated and the number and types of channels to the consumer grows, each company must decide for itself what channels it must use. The sophisticated company uses more than one channel to drive sales.

The last few years have brought this major dilemma to many providers of goods and services. An analysis is necessary to determine the best channels for a company to reach its customer since each channel carries its own advantages and disadvantages and cost/profit structure. Figure 12-1 gives an example.

By putting estimated volume, cost, and profit numbers to the examples I have given, you can develop a distribution matrix that will work for your specific company.

Again, most successful companies today utilize a multichannel approach to the marketplace. My error in operating the distributor-dependent company I mentioned was in assuming that loyalty to members of my distribution chain would garner greater effort on their part, hence greater sales for my company. The truth is that each portion of the channel serves a different purpose and a company should utilize the best mix for its needs.

3. YOUR SALES DEPARTMENT IS NOT EXERCISING
THE PROPER EFFORT

There have been volumes written about motivating a sales force. I wrote about incentive programs in Chapter 6, but at the begin-

FIGURE 12-1 ■ Advantages and Disadvantages of Various Distribution Channels.

Channel	Advantages/Disadvantages	Cost	Profit
1. Own sales force	Control of semifixed cost, including base salary and expenses	Commissions	Good
2. Representative sales force or distributor	No control over day-to-day activities/totally variable cost	Higher commissions or discounts	Fair
3. Internet sales	Direct to customer/low support levels	Cost of website and fulfillment costs	Good
4. Telemarketing	Direct to customer/medium support levels	Cost of telemarketer	Good
5. Television marketing direct to consumer	Direct to customer/medium support/high cost of entry/wide coverage	Cost structure depends on selling network	Fair
6. Retail store	Can have wide distribution/high service levels/high overhead if stores are owned	Cost discounts	Fair

ning of this chapter I stated that my philosophy with sales personnel is now almost entirely based upon their ability to deliver that which is promised.

I have found that the most effective way to drive a sales force is through meticulous call planning and follow-up. By having your sales management develop a system of daily call assignments (which provides a salesperson with a mix of new and existing clients) followed by a reporting system that indicates if the call was made and its results, you can gain control of the process. Today's computer-based systems combined with handheld personal digital assistants has streamlined the control and reporting processes dramatically.

Needless to say, one must hire motivated high-energy sales personnel, but some of the dos and don'ts I have found over the years are:

- Do identify the high-potential accounts in the salesperson's territory.

- Do provide the "story" in either presentation format or brochures for the salesperson to utilize.

- Do provide incentives for salespeople who constantly achieve or exceed their goals.

- Do occasionally travel with sales personnel to meet key customers.

- Don't give sales personnel pricing latitude above certain minimums.

- Do give sales personnel the ability to request competitive pricing from a special pricing committee at headquarters.

- Do provide training, support, and guidance to sales personnel.

- Do be prepared to cull the lowest 10 percent of the performers each year.

All this assumes that you have a dedicated internal sales force; external sales forces such as hired independent representatives and distributors require even more incentives because they are not employees and tend to be unwilling to adhere to the call plan I mentioned earlier. This means constant interaction to ensure that they are following through on suggested call schedules. Again, deliverables are the key. If a distributor or an external representative does not deliver agreed-upon numbers, it is time to ride another horse.

In retail sales, often the sales personnel view themselves as merely order takers and cashiers. One of the retail chains that has raised retail sales to a fine art is Nordstrom®. Its sales personnel suggest items to customers and personally follow through with thank-you notes to customers, alerting them to sales events and items in which they might be interested. They help drive positive sales effort and generate multiple visits to the store. This effort is the result of Nordstrom's keen perception and understanding of its customers and excellent training of its own floor-sales personnel.

4. THERE IS A PROBLEM WITH THE PRODUCT OR SERVICE YOU ARE SELLING

I like to put it this way: There is no amount of pricing that can offset a poor product or an improperly performed service.

One of the first things I examine when I enter a company is the quality of the product or service that is being provided. Often sales are negatively affected by poor quality or technological obsolescence. I will discuss manufacturing for profit in Chapter 14, but for now let's examine the problem of products or services that do not match the consumer's expectations.

I once was called in to turn around a company that had developed a fully automated system for grinding glass lenses for eyeglasses. Unfortunately, a whole new technology—plastic lenses—had emerged and rendered the products obsolete. The owners needed a course of action that would save them extensive capital investment.

I suggested two steps for them to pursue:

1. Sell product that could not be produced in plastic, such as extremely complex optics that were needed on a specialty basis.

2. Begin seeking an alliance with precision-optics companies to produce specialty fine-glass lenses as components of their devices (e.g., cameras, microscopes, and other devices).

It was because the managers could not think outside their traditional markets that they were failing to recognize that their "primary" market was gone forever.

Recently I purchased airline tickets online from a division of my Internet service provider. Something went wrong and I received tickets for a date other than that which I had ordered. When I tried to contact someone who could correct the problem, I kept getting the service desk in India, which was not authorized to provide any assistance of substance and refused to recognize the error on its part. After 16 phone calls I gave up!

Even though the tickets were deeply discounted, I swore that I would never use the service again and would discourage everyone I know from using it as well. In our highly wired world, instant communication allows us to shop many places electronically, but it also allows us to express dissatisfaction to a much broader base than in the past.

There is no more perfect example of this than the restaurant that serves poor-quality food and provides bad service. There are a host of websites rating restaurants, which allows consumers to provide feedback.

So what are the rules? Very simply:

- Ensure that your product or service meets the needs of your identified customer base.

- Ensure that the quality of your goods and services meets the expectations of your customer base.

- Ensure that your product or service is technologically appropriate to the needs of your customers.

Often part of what a turnaround person brings to a company is a realistic evaluation of the goods and services being offered and what needs to be changed. In Chapter 5 I asked you to identify your product's advantages and disadvantages. This analysis can provide clues as to the adequacy of your product offerings.

CHAPTER THIRTEEN

SOURCING AND GLOBALIZATION

If we have learned anything over the last decade it is the global nature of business. Goods and services can and are both bought and sold internationally.

Because the U.S. market is so large and diverse, many foreign producers wish to market their products here, and as a result our balance of payments continues to worsen over time. Unfortunately, I have had to oversee the demise or downsizing of several textile and apparel manufacturing companies whose production costs were too high in comparison to companies in China and Indonesia. In fact, it is estimated that over 200 apparel manufacturers have closed in the United States over the last 20 years with the attendant loss of over one million jobs. In this chapter I will discuss both sourcing from abroad and selling goods and services worldwide.

Because most companies will die and turn to ash long before the U.S. Government will impose protective tariffs on items competitive with U.S. goods, companies must take self-defensive measures to ensure survival. This means that finding the lowest-cost production alternative may require outsourcing.

OUTSOURCING

There are certain industries that out of necessity have learned how to outsource very well and profitably. As I stated, the textile industry was one of the first to go offshore, primarily to China and now to other third-world countries. As one might imagine there is a limit to which one can drive productivity in facilities in order to lower costs and still not offset the rock-bottom wages and benefits paid in certain areas of the world. Let's discuss the advantages and disadvantages of offshore product sourcing.

Advantages

- **Cost.** In extremely low labor-rate areas, it is possible to cut the costs of certain products with a large labor content to 25 to 50 percent of American labor costs. Even with ocean freight, the cost is still lower than U.S.-manufactured goods.

- **Quality.** This can be both an advantage and a disadvantage. Quality on imported goods can be very good; however, if good monitoring systems and standards are not in place, this area can quickly become a disadvantage.

Disadvantages

- **Distance.** Usually there is a significant distance between the source of goods and the user, for example, China and the United States. This then translates into longer shipment time and delivery risk.

- **Cash Flow.** International transactions are usually done on letters of credit (L/Cs), with payment made as the goods are loaded on the ship. This requires committing cash or borrowing capacity to the producer well before you sell the goods.

- **Commitment.** Once the goods are ordered and the L/C is placed, you have made a firm commitment for goods and there is no flexibility as to delivery or quantity.

- **Quality.** Unless quality is monitored well, there is a possibility of shipment of off-quality goods.

- **Litigation.** If a problem arises, it is very difficult to adjudicate differences in foreign courts. Even in developed countries such as Italy or France, it is almost impossible to obtain a timely resolution of issues or to collect judgments.

- **Intellectual Property.** Many countries do not honor U.S. patent protections even when protections have been applied for and received in a foreign country. Again, the ability to adjudicate differences varies greatly from country to country.

- **Fraud.** Another disadvantage of dealing with other countries is fraud in a number of ways. This includes substitution of components that are cheaper, copying of the product, and sale in countries other than the United States.

PRECAUTIONARY MEASURES

Now that I've scared you out of your wits, I need to say that despite all these disadvantages, taking 12 precautionary measures can reduce importation risks to minimal levels.

1. Determine who the best players (sources) are in a given country. This can be done through recommendations from the U.S. Department of Commerce, various trade agencies of the country in which you plan on doing business, and lenders (banks) with correspondent banks in the country in question.

2. Check out the recommended partner you plan on doing business with by obtaining references and visiting it. Also visit its bank and get any available financial data you can on the company. Talk to people in the United States who have done business with the company.

3. Determine if the company's capacity meets your needs in both the short and long term.

4. Determine the level of quality of product you can expect and be prepared to establish a liaison and inspection office in the country from which you will be importing. It is most important that you have a person on-site whom you pay to represent your interests.

5. In your agreement, determine what the economics of your deal will be, including cost of the item or service, cost of liaison and visits, and costs of shipping and insurance so that the real cost of outsourcing is truly understood. Understand the potential risks and allow for them in your economic calculations; for example, allow for one or two extra shipments a year to cover late shipments or delays.

6. Explore more than one vendor in the country that you plan to source from, and have possible alternate sources outside the target country in case of political instability.

7. In your agreement, have safeguards as to delivery, quality, and cost, and have your letters of credit incorporate these items in order to allow you to withhold payment if conditions are not met.

8. Ensure that any L/Cs are on a U.S. bank with which you have a good relationship in the event of problems.

9. Use the best freight forwarder you can find and get it to help you negotiate shipping rates.

10. Check on incoming tariffs and duties as part of your economics calculation. In some instances, it is better to import components and conduct final assembly in the United States to avoid excessive duties on finished product.

11. Be very cognizant of local laws and customs regarding employment of individuals and the cost of changing or terminating a relationship. For example, the cost of terminating an employee in France is very onerous compared with that in many other countries.

12. Be sure that the lead times for ordering product are consistent with your customers' needs and that having an offshore production facility does not hamper your sales. Long lead times may cause you to hold inventory in the United States, adding another set of costs to the economics of importation.

Despite any disadvantages and corollary precautions, outsourcing can be very lucrative and allow a company to compete very effectively in its marketplace.

EXPORTING

It has only been in the last two decades that U.S. companies have begun to export in earnest. There are a few multinational companies, such as Coca-Cola®, that were well known for their exporting expertise, but for the most part U.S. companies have been content to sell primarily to the vast U.S. markets and haven't focused on their ability to sell goods and services abroad. Today the Internet allows one to do business with the world at large. However, you must do several things to enhance your ability to sell products and services outside the United States. The following seven tips can help when considering exporting a product or service:

1. Each country has a unique culture and language, and these have to be considered when thinking about sales.

2. Strategic market research is necessary to determine the best places to go with your product. This is especially important because of the initial cost of establishing markets in various countries.

3. Just as in importing, political stability and local economic conditions affect the size and viability of a market and the ability of the locals to purchase your product or service.

4. Different duties and restrictive barriers to commerce exist in various countries, and these local conditions often act as economic barriers to exporting product.

5. Freight costs may play a part in determining pricing and the economics of selling abroad.

6. The cost of collecting receivables from foreign purchasers can be problematic if one is not careful. As I stated in the outsourcing section of this chapter, if you are attempting to collect from delinquent accounts in foreign courts, know that these courts are generally not friendly to U.S. companies that don't normally play on their turf.

7. Exchange rates add a level of complexity to pricing and gross margin that one does not face in domestic sales.

Given all this, the global opportunities are virtually limitless if one plans carefully. Think of the huge markets in China and Eastern Europe, where there is demand for products and services that have not developed there. For example, fast-food companies such as McDonald's and KFC recognized many years ago that there was a demand for economically priced convenient food in countries other than the United States, and they began to export the concept. I once ran a company that did 60 percent of its business outside the United States, and some of our most profitable items were products designed for the European and Asian markets.

There are huge mistakes that companies can make when they fail to take cultural differences into account. For instance, I once tried to export electric wheelchairs into Japan. I thought they would be a slam dunk because Japan was a high-population-density country with great regard for its elderly and infirm. In addition, Japanese consumers could afford what I wanted to export. But I discovered after several rather expensive visits that the Japanese want to take care of the infirm—at home. They don't want them zipping around the streets in motorized conveyances. Illness or infirmity is considered a private problem, and I was attempting to put the lame and infirm out on the street for all to see, violating cultural taboos. Oops! Things may have changed in Japan in the ensuing years, but I really don't think so.

TIPS ON EXPORTING

So how do you get into the export business, and even better, make money at it? Here are 11 tips:

1. **First, pick your markets.** Just as you analyzed strategic markets in Chapter 3, you must pick the markets where there is demand for your goods or services. Alternatively, companies can create demand where there is minimal or unsophisticated competition.

2. **Study the barriers to entry, such as tariffs and government regulations.** In certain countries where there is a national policy to develop, for example, steel production, there may be huge tariffs and volume restrictions on imported steel (actually the United States did this until recently).

For example, I once tried to export an electronic beverage-dispensing device to Japan. There was nothing like it being made in Japan at the time and I thought we would have smooth sailing. However, when it came to getting approval from the Ministry of Industry and Trade (MITI), we were informed that we needed to install a rather expensive ground-fault detector on our device so that people using it would not get electrocuted. We protested because the ground-fault detector was going to cost as much as the product and would make it too expensive to sell. Because of the low voltages involved, the probablility of electrocution was virtually nil.

The MITI officials told us that if we were to "team up" with a Japanese company, they would waive the need for this device. I then asked how "teaming up" reduced the probability of electrocution and was told that because a Japanese company would now stand behind this product the government would be confident that no one would get hurt. It was a very obvious nontariff barrier that was being placed in our path. We eventually signed a joint agreement with a Japanese company that was agreeable to all, including MITI.

3. **Obtain reputable sales representatives in the country of choice.** Or open your own sales office and hire locals to operate it. For some period of time have someone from your home office present to supervise and train the personnel. This is especially important if the local language is not English.

4. **Prepare your sales documents and product literature in the language of the country that your market is in.** This seems obvious, but one of the biggest failings of U.S. companies is to recognize

that providing instructions in English to non-English-speaking countries is not only silly but an open insult. The suppliers of computer and other electronic equipment have learned this lesson and have prepared almost all their documentation in multiple language formats.

If you are just starting to export product and are uncomfortable with the expense of multilanguage literature and the preparation needed for certain countries, then start out only in English-speaking countries such as Australia, England, Scotland, and Ireland. Remember that these countries have some cultural diversity as well.

5. **Be prepared to deal with time differences in servicing accounts in different parts of the world.** People don't care that the United States may be 6 or even 12 hours behind. They need help in their workday, not yours.

6. **Adjust your method of receivables collection to reflect the added risk associated with foreign sales.** For example, use letters of credit where you can (use accredited banks). Back sales or credit up with personal guarantees where possible.

7. **Ensure that trademarks and patents are filed in the countries in which you plan to do business.** I have heard horror stories about trade names being stolen in countries where the exporter failed to register a name.

8. **Capitalize on employer-friendly countries.** Establish offices and warehouses in countries where the employment laws do not unduly penalize you if you wish to change personnel or move an office.

9. **Treat the foreign offices as "part of the team," communicate with them, and visit them**

regularly. As I mentioned, telecommunications is at the point where regular videoconferences are inexpensive. Watch their spending and resultant sales just as you would any U.S. office.

10. **Set pricing of the product in the currency of the country or the region.** Some of my worst fights with foreign distributors were over the change in the value of the U.S. dollar compared with the euro and what it did to affect our pricing. Adjust pricing every three to six months, but use the local currency.

11. **Watch your back.** Obtain adequate risk insurance for the operation of these foreign operations.

Again, all this sounds tough, but international sales can be rewarding and a lot of fun.

CHAPTER FOURTEEN

SPECIAL ANALYSIS TOOLS

In this chapter I will discuss two special tools that are useful in any company of any size. They are:

1. Cash flow analysis

2. Value analysis

Cash flow analysis is the forward-looking radar that allows a company to adjust its monetary strategies to allow for cash flow fluctuations and bumps in the business environment. Value analysis allows a company to adjust its products or services to meet its customers' expectations while minimizing cost and maximizing quality.

Both are very important and amazingly underutilized in business.

CASH FLOW—THE LIFEBLOOD OF A COMPANY

Suppose I was your physician and I told you that I couldn't stop the bleeding from a wound and had no way to replenish your blood supply. You would panic because you would know that you were going to die. The same is true for cash in a company. Cash flow is the blood that keeps the company going and without it a company withers and dies. Yet it is amazing how few companies attempt to predict their cash flow and take steps to ensure that they don't run out of cash at a critical time.

A horror story I experienced early in my career occurred while I was executive VP and chief operating officer of an extremely large integrated petroleum refiner and marketing company. The company had embarked on an extremely large construction project for the manufacture of a new chemical product. The CEO was very entrepreneurial in nature and not a great economic analyst.

In the process of managing the construction of the new plant, as one of my duties I was planning manpower requirements and determined that we would have 1,200 construction personnel on site. I did a quick calculation of cash flow from operations and determined that we would run out of cash in three months if we didn't presell product or arrange for external financing.

I called this problem to the attention of the CEO and was told that my job was to see that the construction came in "on time" and "on budget" and that he would take care of the financing. Three months later we ran out of cash and declared bankruptcy.

To a bank, one of the first signs that a company has poor management is its inability to predict and plan for cash needs. Typical companies that find themselves in cash crunches are:

- Start-ups and new ventures

- Rapidly growing companies

- Companies undertaking mergers or acquisitions

- Companies undergoing large new-product development programs

- Companies whose customers are undergoing economic stress

Let's address each in turn.

START-UPS AND NEW VENTURES

These companies will typically underestimate the amount of cash and time it takes to get the enterprise going. Unanticipated expenses coupled with slower than expected revenue growth are the primary reasons these companies find the coffers dry. Entrepreneurs are by their very nature optimistic as to the success of their new baby and fail to consider downsides adequately. Some examples of this are:

- **Slow Growth.** Many start-ups will take two to three times as long to ramp up sales as the entrepreneur anticipated. A sure sign of overenthusiastic growth projections are "hockey stick" growth curves in which sales take off at fantastic rates, whereas in the real world there is often great initial resistance to new products and it takes time to get past this "start-up" period.

- **Unanticipated Expenses.** There are often unanticipated expenses, such as legal costs or personnel costs, that are higher than planned for. These costs are exacerbated by slow growth since there is no revenue to offset them. A good example of this is the cost of new salespeople who are not productive for several months while continuing to run up salaries and expenses.

The solution to the entrepreneur's natural optimism is to perform a number of projections of cash flow under a number of "what if" scenarios, quantifying the effect of adverse situations.

Some of these "what if" scenarios might include:

- Taking twice as long to start up as expected
- Slower than projected growth rates
- Increasing start-up costs
- Providing contingencies for unquantified costs
- Higher than expected production costs

Thus, you can develop a "best- and worst-case scenario" and plan for enough cash to cover several or at least one or two pessimistic situations.

RAPIDLY GROWING COMPANIES

It has been said that almost as many companies fail because of overly rapid or unanticipated growth as fail because of poor business environments. This is true because companies in a rapid growth mode need cash to cover inventory, receivables, people, and systems growth in advance. Failure to react and move to attract cash in the form of borrowing or equity can lead to an inability to deliver goods or services or a failure to sustain operations.

The cost of an emergency cash bailout can be very large, in both actual dollars and the dilution of equity for the owners. In other words, it is better to negotiate for cash needs when there is no emergency going on. Fire insurance is much less expensive before there is a fire in progress.

Cash projection is essential once the first indications of rapid growth in a sector of the business are seen. If you create a cash projection that shows that you need significant cash in the future in order to grow, you should immediately plan for it. Most traditional lending institutions, such as banks, are willing to support growth in a business they are familiar and comfortable with. There are also a number of asset-based lenders (ABLs) that are willing to support growth in receivables and inventory. A frank discussion with your lender will determine the best route for your business.

Another approach is to enhance your cash position by selling bonds or other debt instruments that can be used to support growth. And, finally, there are companies, such as investment funds, that are willing to invest in businesses that show growth potential.

The point of all this is that it takes time to raise money. A cash projection gives you the warning signals that cash will be required in the future and that you had better take action to get it or take steps to conserve cash until a solution can be found.

COMPANIES UNDERTAKING MERGERS
OR ACQUISITIONS

Even with the best planning, mergers or acquisitions cost more than anticipated. Just as in the start-up or new-venture situation, risk and Murphy's Law are in full play—the problems of timing, or failures to rationalize cost can affect cash flow. There are always snags and legal bumps in the road to overcome. Again a "what if" scenario and cash flow need to be developed to recognize these modifications in plans and a strategy must be developed to deal with each in turn.

I was involved with a public company that was merging with a nonpublic company. The intent was that the two companies would be merged within six months, including all Securities and Exchange Commission (SEC) approvals, etc. Due to negotiations, lawyers' comments, SEC responses, changes in business structure, and other things, the process took over a year and a half and ran up $500,000 in lawyers' costs that were not expected. We very fortunately had anticipated some of these events in a "worst-case scenario" cash flow, but we still hadn't anticipated all the extra cash flow. Because of forward cash flow planning we were able to get through the cash crunch.

COMPANIES UNDERGOING LARGE NEW-
PRODUCT DEVELOPMENT PROGRAMS

Most development programs are late and cost more than initially budgeted. Please excuse my pessimism but I have seen this happen far too often not to anticipate the event. By planning for a delay and its attendant costs one can often avoid returning to the cash source over and over again. For the most part, I address this problem in Chapter 16, on research and development.

I will usually create a cash flow that reflects adding three to six months to a development project, plus some additional costs associated with the delay. The greatest effect from a slowed new-product launch is the delay of expected revenues and profits from the new product. Often you can "hedge your bets" by holding back on pre-launch expenditures until certain key milestones are reached that indicate that the new product or service is ready for market. As in the other areas, the cash flow projection shows both the impact of a later launch and the cash needs for a product introduction.

COMPANIES WHOSE CUSTOMERS ARE UNDERGOING ECONOMIC STRESS

This is a broad category that affects every business at one time or another. What if your customer fails to pay you or, in the worst case, goes bankrupt and you lose a receivable? Or economic conditions take a downturn and everyone begins to pay slower than anticipated? What can you do? What happens to your cash flow? Usually these conditions do not manifest themselves suddenly and thus you have some time, although limited, in which to do cash flow projections and take corrective actions.

The really helpful thing about cash flow analysis is that it allows you to examine your cash receipts from each of your customers on a realistic basis. This forces management to reexamine receivables by customer to see which ones are perennial slow payers and which ones are in trouble based on their payment patterns. Then you can enter their payments on the cash flow schedule at the time you really expect to receive them. This exercise sets off alarms as to those customers you really have to "work with" to bring in cash and those who provide the greatest risk of default.

At a company I worked with not too long ago, there was a large customer that began paying its bills later and later. Its late payments began having an adverse effect on cash flow. I began making discreet inquiries and found that it was having financial difficulties unrelated to our business. I worked out a payment schedule for it that would allow it to get us "caught up" on the amounts it owed us and eventually put it on a cash on delivery (C.O.D.) basis. Unfortunately, it declared Chapter 11, but it was eventually able to reorganize. (We continued to provide product on a C.O.D. basis during the bankruptcy.) Most of the customer's pre-petition suppliers were hurt severely, recovering only cents on the dollar of pre-petition receivables. However, we were not only kept whole, but were able to continue to service the account.

In summary, every company, both big and small, should be performing cash flow projections to manage its most precious resource—money. Cash flow projections will tell you when to borrow money, when to invest money, and when to seek money from your customers. It should be used with the other tools provided in this book to guide you through that jungle out there called business.

CASH PROJECTIONS

Here are some instructions on how to do cash projections.

In troubled situations a bank will typically ask the borrower for a 13-week projection, since this covers a full quarter. This is a useful standard period of time, but you will want to carry it further so that you have a longer view of the future and more options as to corrective action. I suggest the following:

- A 13-week projection by week

- The balance of the year (nine months) performed by month

- The projection should be updated monthly adding four or five weeks of detail for the front end and one new month to the full year of projections. For example, if you have January, February, and March by week, you can do the balance of the year through December by month. Then, the next month you should have February, March, and April by week and May through January by month.

- Remember that a cash projection is not a profit and loss statement. It reflects what is left in the cigar box in cash or cash equivalents at the end of the month. You may have the most profitable company in the world yet may be bleeding cash due to capital expenditures or investments in inventory.

Let's examine each item on the cash flow schedule (Figure 14-1).

STARTING CASH

Starting cash is the actual cash in the bank including short-term accessible cash. If a company has cash that may be an asset but is not accessible such as an investment in another company that is not liquid, it is of no use in the cash flow analysis. This number is also the net cash number from the end of the previous month.

SOURCES OF CASH

This category represents all the places that cash is expected to come from in the weeks and months in the future and contains items such as receipts.

"Receipts" is a compilation by customer or source of payments to the company and when they are expected to be received. Thus, if a customer is always slow to pay, a realistic estimate of the amount and timing of the payments should be utilized, or if a customer is on a "work out" payment schedule, this schedule should be inserted. A separate schedule outlining customer payments by week is often helpful so that the summary cash flow is not overly long.

"Interest" reflects any interest income from investments by the company and when they expect to be received.

FIGURE 14-1 ■ Cash Flow Schedule.

Month	1	1	1	1	2	2	2	2	3	3	3	3
Week	1	2	3	4	1	2	3	4	1	2	3	4
A) Starting Cash												
SOURCES OF CASH												
◆ Receipts												
◆ Interest												
◆ sale of assets												
◆ other												
B) Subtotal (sources)												
USES OF CASH												
◆ Payroll												
◆ Taxes												
◆ Operating Expenses												
◆ Material Purchases												
◆ Equipment Expenditures												
◆ Repairs												
◆ Loans/Bank Payments												
◆ Bonuses												
◆ Other Disbursements												
C) Subtotal (uses)												
USABLE CASH (D)												
A + B − C = D												
Borrowing												
New Equity												
NET CASH (to starting cash)												

"Sale of Assets" is the net cash received from the sale of any asset of the company such as cars, buildings, and scrap.

"Other" is any source of funds other than new borrowings or new equity that is covered later in the schedule.

USES OF CASH

The uses of cash category is a summary of all the expected expenditures of the company by category. I have given some examples of items but not an all-inclusive list, which will vary by company. It is important to place the expenditures in the schedule at the time you expect them to be paid.

"Payroll," "Taxes," and most operating expenses usually can be predicted with some accuracy. Material purchases should be predicted and are dependent on production needs. Capital expenditures need to be inserted since we are concerned with cash—not depreciation. Bank payments and interest are also important in the schedule. Also any loans to officers, bonuses, and other disbursements are required to be entered including nonliquid investments.

★   ★   ★

In this short description of the process I can't cover all the possible items, but they include any use of funds that take them out of the company. By adding "starting cash" and "sources of cash" and by subtracting "uses of cash," one obtains the cash that is available for the company to use at the end of the week.

If there is a deficit there has to be an injection of funds either through borrowing or new equity to cover the shortfall. If there is an excess, a decision needs to be made as to what to do with the excess if it is significant.

CASH SURPLUS

Having large cash surpluses can be dealt with in the following ways:

- Investment in interest-bearing instruments

- Purchase of assets for the company

- Buying back stock

- Distribution to the ownership (dividends)

- Bonuses to the employees

- Reduction in debt

You can easily see that through this method it rapidly becomes obvious if a company needs a long-term cash source to solve an emerging problem.

Most of what I just proposed can be facilitated through the use of a computer but it does require intelligent input from the chief financial officer and continuing dialogue with the various department heads.

Examples of this would be finding out:

- When and how much needs to be spent on repair and refurbishment costs (e.g., a new roof for the plant or overhauling a piece of machinery)?

- When does obsolete equipment need to be replaced and what is the cost?

- Are there any unusual one-time costs that the company will see in the near future? How much will they be?

- Are there any expected litigation costs or settlements in the near future?

- Are there any tax refunds or insurance claims that are due? When are they due and how much are they?

You would be amazed at how many of these items come to light when they are discussed in preparing the cash flow projection. Really well-managed companies utilize cash flow projection techniques as part of their tool belt.

Again, remember it is okay to seek borrowing or equity to support well-planned growth. It is not okay to seek funds to support cash flow surprises and reflects poorly on management when it happens.

VALUE ANALYSIS—EXAMINING PRODUCTS TO LOWER COSTS

A very effective way to lower product costs is through a technique known as value analysis. There are many other names for the value analysis technique, such as "design for manufacturing" or "product line optimization." This methodology requires that you know several things about the marketplace prior to performing the exercise. These are:

- How is my product/service perceived in terms of quality and performance?

- What is the expectation of the marketplace with regard to features and functionality?

- Where do my products sit in their technological life cycle? Do they need to be improved?

- How do I compare with the competition in terms of cost?

This method of reducing costs often meets resistance, just like niche pricing does, due to the misconception that any attempt to change the product will cheapen it and reduce quality.

In almost every instance of value analysis you will exit the process with a higher-quality, better product that is less costly to make.

I once ran a company that produced a complex electronic printing device that took 10 to 12 man-hours to produce and over a week to wend its way through our manufacturing process. When we were done with the value analysis, the product took less than 2 man-hours to produce and moved through the manufacturing floor in less than a day.

Now don't be deceived. This value process took a lot of work and considerable investment in specialized tooling to achieve, but in the end it was well worth it.

Start by laying the product out in component form on a table or on the factory floor in front of a team comprising all the disciplines that affect the cost of the unit, such as marketing, engineering, purchasing, manufacturing, and accounting. Then begin to ask questions such as:

- What is this unit supposed to do?

- What parts are extraneous to the purpose of this device?

- What parts do we manufacture? Can we outsource them cheaper?

- What parts are outsourced? Can we manufacture them cheaper?

- What parts are available in standard sizes that we now use in volume that can be substituted for components of the unit (screws and fasteners are a favorite item here)?

- What major components can be purchased more cheaply in standard sizes from another supplier?

- What manufacturing technique can be modified to make the unit easier to produce?

- What features would we change to improve the product?

- What components can be made of less expensive materials?

- Can we combine or integrate components to reduce cost?

- What tools would make the unit easier to assemble and what components should be changed to accommodate that tooling?

- What can be done to maximize the quality and reliability of the product without adding to cost?

- What components are overdesigned in view of the expected life of the product?

- What new technologies can be brought to bear to update the product?

- What can be done to visually update the product?

- Can the size of the product be changed to make it less costly to ship?

- How can we reduce the parts count in this device to the absolute minimum?

The responsibility for answering these questions is then assigned to the team you have assembled. There should be a team leader who coordinates the efforts of the group. Several meetings of the team will be needed per product studied until an action plan emerges. A sample action plan format would look like Figure 14-2.

You will be amazed by the results of this effort and the amount of money you can save by employing this technique across your product line.

In the area of services, the way you perform a task, the various people involved, and the reduction of complexity should be part of the value analysis.

Hospitals, for example, have been forced to reexamine the way they provide services in an environment of rapidly changing needs and imposed regulations.

They must go through a value analysis process every year or less to determine if they are economically delivering their services at a profit, and if not, they must adjust their method of operation accordingly. Unfortunately, many hospitals don't do this and fail or rely on contributions to continue their efforts.

The value analysis technique should be used for each old product and certainly every new product at least once a year. You will soon find that many of the parts in your product line are inter-

FIGURE 14-2 ■ Sample Action Plan Format.

Product: _____

Component	Current Cost	Proposed Action	Estimated Savings/Unit		Required Investment	Estimated Timing
			Labor	Cost		

changeable and that your raw materials inventory will begin to shrink.

In fact, I found that people were beginning to think of borrowing components from existing models of products as a base of design for new product. This led to modularization and attendant savings.

Savings of as much as 10 to 50 percent in the cost of a product or service can be achieved by this process but it requires cooperation among the members of the team.

One of the areas of greatest sensitivity is purchasing and the willingness of this function to reexamine the cost of each and every component. The greatest resistance I have received in the value analysis effort has come from this area due to the immense amount of work that this process takes.

As a practical matter, it may make sense to devote a dedicated purchasing agent to this effort alone. This, of course, is dependent on the number and complexity of your product line or service.

CHAPTER FIFTEEN

PRODUCTIVITY

This chapter is devoted to companies that manufacture a product and want to do it better. We all manufacture something. Service companies really manufacture an intellectual product that uses many of the elements of the manufacturing process. Fixing broken and wounded production processes may mean manufacturing a physical item such as an automobile or producing a legal presentation for use in court. What elements are common to both manufacturing industries and service industries?

- **Physical Plant.** Both manufacturing and service businesses must have physical facilities to operate out of. Both offices and plants must be managed and maintained.

- **People.** All types of businesses need people to generate their products, and their productivity affects profitability greatly.

- **Materials and Assets.** Manufacturing uses material and machinery to fabricate products. Service businesses use some materials, supplies, and machinery in the form of computers and other specialized devices to deliver their product.

- **Overhead.** Both operations have supervision and overhead items such as insurance and consumables.

- **Financial and Production Controls.** Both operations use money, spend it, and need to control it.

So you can see that most of the elements in manufacturing are common to service businesses. Let's discuss each in turn.

PHYSICAL PLANT

When I go into a plant or office I can usually tell you within five minutes if it is a smooth-flowing facility, how productive and efficient people are, and the general morale of the employees.

The first thing I look for is cleanliness and organization. A dirty, run-down facility screams of inefficiency and lack of caring on the part of management and staff. A cluttered office sends exactly the same kind of message. I look for flow and a plan of moving either product or paper from place to place. I look for indications of productivity and employee feedback.

The first thing that I do in a dirty facility is clean it up. I'm not talking about major renovations or moving production to make it more efficient. I'm talking about soap, water, paint, and wax. This accomplishes several things very rapidly:

- It says that a new force is at work in the facility and more changes are to come.

- To the employees it says "take pride in your work."

- It lifts employee morale as well as employee productivity.

Special places to clean up are the restrooms and dining areas, since we all must use these facilities daily. These are the areas that can cause the greatest irritation to employees if they are not clean and can make the greatest impression if they are clean and bright.

A second sign that a plant is running well is "pace." That is, if there is a "hum" of production, if most of the machines are in use, if there is activity—these are all signs of an efficient, well-run facility.

The third element of a well-run facility is smiles on the faces of the employees. If they are glum and unresponsive when management walks through a plant, there is a problem. If they say hi and are happily engaged in tasks, then you can be sure that morale is high.

A very rapid measure of productivity in a plant or an office is to count the number of people in a given area and to determine through observation how many of them are actually performing a productive activity. The ratio of people who are really "doing something" to the total number is often a shocker. It is usually in the 50 percent or lower range; the objective should be to get it above 70 percent.

PHYSICAL LAYOUT

The physical layout of the facilities should follow the natural flow of the products being manufactured, and in an office, the natural flow of paperwork. The idea is to make the flow as efficient as possible and reduce handling and labor to the greatest degree achievable. There are specialists who can help you with plant layout and installation of movement facilitators such as conveyor belts and automated handling systems.

These methods will vary widely, depending on the products you make, the volume you produce, and the economics of the process. Obviously one would not install a highly automated production line to make a very customized product in small quantities. Conversely, one would be crazy to manufacture a high-volume product by hand.

The real first step in producing anything efficiently is to reexamine the product itself and see if it lends itself to ease of production. This is called "product optimization" or "designs for manufacturing" and is deceptively simple. But before I go into the process, let's talk about how most products get designed. First an idea for a new product is given to the company's research and development department, which then sees if it can make a reasonable prototype of the product.

Now in making this prototype, the engineer or scientist isn't particularly concerned with the cost or manufacturability of the product—all he wants to do is get something that works, so he may use very expensive components and he probably doesn't care that it is unwieldy to put together.

In the next step, once the concept has been proved, engineers get the product into a producible form. At this stage, they may modify the product design to make it more useable and producible. They then begin to work with purchasing to determine where components can be purchased at the lowest cost. The company then purchases the tools to produce the product, it sets up the production lines, and it launches the product.

The only problem with all of this is that in reality, except in the most sophisticated of companies, there is such time pressure to launch the product that it never gets optimized. In Chapter 14, I described a value analysis technique to correct this error and save money in the process. It is very effective and should be utilized.

MACHINERY AND EQUIPMENT

In my earlier book I described in great detail a method of justifying new investments through their economic return on the capital invested. A ranking of these investments based on the highest return first gives a company a guide as to the priority of the investments. This is just sound business and most good companies employ this technique today. However, I have modified the game with several techniques that turnaround advisers use and are applicable to any company. These methods allow one to justify capital investment by lowering the cost of equipment and hence shortening the payback time. Since turnaround experts seldom have enough cash to make the investments they need, they must improvise. Some of these methods are as follows:

- **Refurbish and upgrade existing equipment.**
  Many times existing equipment can be upgraded or modernized at much lower cost than purchasing new equipment.

- **Buy used equipment.** The cost of used equipment is usually 50 to 80 percent less than new equipment of the same type. It is usually not as sophisticated as the latest version but makes up for its lower productivity in terms of cost.

- **Trade in old equipment for new equipment from the same vendor.** Some vendors will give generous trade-in allowances for their old equipment in order to keep a customer. I have used this method effectively with vendors.

- **Structure better payment or lease deals.**
  Equipment vendors will stretch payment terms to acceptable limits, thus shifting the burden of technological obsolescence back to the vendor in a short-term renewable lease (this is often done in computer purchases).

All of these methods reduce risk as well as cost for the company.

PEOPLE

Possibly the most important element of manufacturing is people. They are your most important asset, and getting people to operate at their most efficient level is a major consideration in any company.

In Chapter 6, I wrote about communications and how to keep everyone in a company informed. Now I want to tackle a specific area of people relations: motivating and rewarding those in the production area.

INCENTIVE PROGRAMS

Over the years, I have worked with numerous financial and non-financial incentives for production personnel and I think I have come up with a method that has really worked. I have used it often and it appears to be a win-win for the company and the employees. It combines incentives for output, quality, and attendance.

It first involves setting standards for what the labor component of the production of a product should be. In other words, if assembly should take 20 minutes, then that is the standard per unit of production. This is achieved through testing and measurement by standard industrial-engineering techniques.

The second step is to divide the company into incentive teams in which output can be measured. For example, one assembly line plus its supervisors and support personnel (such as material handlers) compose a team. Then you can implement a group incentive for each team that generates 25 to 50 percent labor savings when its output goes over 90 percent of the standard. These savings go into a pool and accumulate each quarter. Defective output and rework is deducted from the pool. Overtime premiums also reduce the labor savings. At the end of a quarter, the pool is distributed among the employees based on the number of hours they worked during the quarter compared with the total hours worked by the team.

For example, if Mary Jane takes three sick days and seven vacation days during a quarter, the others on the team have to cover for her and make up 80 extra hours during the quarter. Say there are five members on the team and the whole team works 2,400 hours during the quarter. Now suppose there is $500 in the pool at the end of the quarter. Normally, Mary Jane would receive one fifth of the pool. But because she only worked 400 out of a possible 480 hours, she would only get 83.3 percent of her normal payout. The other members of the team share the balance.

As a matter of improving their output, the team meets weekly to develop ideas and suggestions—for example, tooling improvement or the quality of component provided to them. The team feeds these suggestions back to plant management, which must keep the team abreast of improvement actions taken. Thus, in one program we have:

- An incentive for improved output

- A quality-control feedback system

- An attendance program

If the program is working well, it yields incentive payments of $0–$200 per quarter per employee. However, it is important that all production is tracked and posted so that employees can see their daily results. It is also the responsibility of plant management to ensure that line loading and production plans do not hinder the productivity program.

"Now," you say, "this program only works in a factory environment." But as I mentioned, I once ran an outdoor-sign company and applied the same techniques to our sign change-out crews and sign-painting crews; it was very successful.

Some of the side benefits of such a program are:

- The teams become self-policing of underperformers or slackers.

- The teams are quick to identify vendors that may be providing parts that may be slightly off specifications.

- The teams provide great input as to methods of production improvement.

These methods, combined with other forms of communication, can generate an enthusiastic workforce. I have also used the incentives to create a bit of competition among teams and have awarded the superteam of the quarter with extra incentives such as gift certificates or free lunches to keep the excitement in the program.

THE UNION

I am often asked, "How do you handle union situations?" or "How do you treat unions?" I treat unions the same way I would treat any other employees: as fairly as I can. I recognize the union when I enter a facility and meet with its representatives when I am trying to fix a company. Since a company's employees may have chosen to have a union represent them, I will always try to enlist the union's aid in improving a company's profitability. I try to get the union to understand the company's problems and conversely I try to understand the union's problems.

Because a union is a representative organization, it has internal political dynamics that management must understand. I tend to communicate with unions as much as I do with the employees and try to minimize surprises. There will be differences of opinion, but the key is to minimize the "us versus them" gulf that can develop in union environments.

MATERIALS AND ASSETS

Another key to manufacturing is material costs. The purchasing department can play a key role in reducing product costs. Unfortunately, often the purchasing function becomes complacent or just plain lazy and fails to police its vendors. Companies tend to buy from the same vendors because they become comfortable with them and tend not to review costs on a regular basis. There are two rules that I enforce in a company with regard to purchases. They are:

1. Always get competitive bids at least once a year.

2. Always have at least one other source of the same item lined up in the event the primary supplier has problems.

This seems almost elementary in concept, but many companies fail to do this because of time constraints and personal relationships. This applies to purchased services as well as materials.

I was once operating a facility that manufactured large-diameter pipe for water transmission. We had been losing money at this particular plant and wanted to find ways to reduce costs. One of the services we purchased was from a company that utilized spray guns (usually used for applying gunite to swimming pools) to apply an even coat of concrete on the outside of the pipe. We had bid the work out, and the purchasing department had determined that this particular vendor provided the most consistent high-quality coating. After some negotiation, the purchasing department struck a deal with the vendor.

In examining the costs, I found that this particular vendor represented $4 million out of $22 million in total costs. I asked the members of the purchasing team if they felt there was any room for negotiation with the vendor, and they told me that the vendor had given its best price. I then sat down and calculated what I thought the vendor's costs in people, equipment, and materials to do our job were. No matter how I calculated the costs, I calculated that the vendor was getting a huge profit on the job while we were struggling to break even.

Against the purchasing department's advice, I called on the vendor and told him that I felt that unless he was using Ph.D.s as workers and was applying special high-end concrete on my pipe, he was dramatically overpriced. I indicated that although we were pleased with his work we needed to rebid the job and, in fact, I was meeting with other vendors that day to obtain quotes and would like him to rebid his work as well. He asked me what kind of reduction in price I would anticipate, and I said 50 percent (which left him with a 15 percent profit according to my calculations). He called back within hours and dropped his price to $2 million for the rest of the job. I later found out that his company, near bankruptcy, was back from the brink by virtue of the high profit we were paying. Needless to say, I replaced my purchasing agent for not doing his homework and I saved $2 million on the job.

I recommend having the accounting department rank all company purchases in descending dollar amount so that the purchasing department can attack the highest-cost items first and work its way down the list. By targeting annual savings goals for the purchasing group and providing economic incentives that will reward achieving and exceeding those goals, I have been able to reduce costs of materials 2–3 percent on a regular basis.

One must have controls in place to ensure that the purchasing department is unable to substitute lower-quality components without the engineering department's approval or purchase of overly large quantities in order to bring prices down.

The cost-review process in purchasing is unending and it is most important to have your best negotiators in this function, especially if your company is material-intensive from a cost standpoint.

In many businesses a company will treat its vendors in an adversarial manner and will attempt to squeeze them for every single penny that they can get. This has resulted in the demise of many suppliers. I believe that mutually beneficial arrangements are the best way to operate.

I have written gain-sharing arrangements into vendor contracts where the vendor and my client company will share in any cost-saving innovations that either side comes up with. This arrangement has yielded some significant results over the long term.

As I stated, the approach I usually take with material vendors applies to service vendors as well. I will discuss treating your banker as a vendor in Chapter 17.

OVERHEAD

There are primarily two types of factory overhead. They are people, in the form of supervisors, and hard assets such as machinery and buildings. The turnaround manager attempts to minimize these costs through various means. Let's examine some of them.

PEOPLE

By using working lead personnel and providing group incentives, I have found that I am usually able to get away with fewer pure supervisors. In businesses with highly seasonal sales, I try to make the staff variable and utilize temporary personnel in the positions that do not require extensive training. Often I will outsource engineering or other technical activities on a specific project-by-project basis when a full-time effort is not required.

EQUIPMENT AND FACILITIES

Most people consider equipment and facilities costs fixed. But the difference between turnaround management and normal management is that turnaround managers realize there are really no true fixed costs. We can take the following actions:

- Renegotiate rents and leases.

- Sell or sublease idle facilities.

- Sell and then lease back facilities to generate cash.

In other words, everything is negotiable. Turnaround people have the advantage of a "crisis" situation to drive such renegotiations, but any company can do the same thing.

I was once involved with a large retail chain with numerous mall locations and fixed-term leases. The chain was not achieving the profits it should and the major problem was subperforming locations. We created a team to renegotiate leases and work with landlords to swap or resize sites. In each location there was a quid pro quo that would work for both the landlord and the company. By extending the terms of the lease or by changing the basis for the rents, we were able to change the paradigm.

I'm not saying it works in every instance, but it is always a worthwhile endeavor.

SAFETY

Injuries in facilities and lost time are major sources of cost to the company and of course a major problem for employees. Every company needs an equal emphasis on employee safety, and a review of those methods and devices needed to keep employees safe and healthy is part of every company's operations.

I will never hesitate to spend money to ensure that employees have the proper safety equipment and that the correct safeguards are in place to ensure that the workplace is safe as well. Conversely, I feel that one of the great dangers to safety is the abuse of substances by employees. In every company I have worked in, I have made a no-tolerance, mandatory drug-and-alcohol testing program an integral part of our employment physical.

In a company I ran in California, the reject rate on new employee applicants due to positive drug-test results was over 50 percent. This did not include those who withdrew from consideration after being warned that they would be rejected for drug use. In one instance, an applicant substituted animal urine for his own in the test. I had a bittersweet laugh when I thought of him chasing his dog around the yard for a sample. A final note: Where there is drug usage, there is usually theft to support the habit (I will get into this in Chapter 18).

FINANCIAL AND PRODUCTION CONTROLS

There are opportunities today through the use of relatively inexpensive devices and computer programs to control what we call the supply chain. Bar codes or radio-frequency tags can track supplies and materials, aid in usage analyses that improve ordering frequency, and track product and costs at various stages of manufacture. Finished goods can be tracked in real time. Shipments can be tracked to the customer. These systems can then be integrated with accounting systems to generate both financial and production reports.

In Chapter 11 I made suggestions as to systems that match each company's needs and result in very rapid paybacks. In any company that handles any significant amount of product, these tracking and control methods will save or prevent:

- Inventory shrinkage

- Overinflation of material costs and quantities

- Shipping losses

I am continually amazed by companies that have not taken advantage of these technological advances. In any case, here are some reports that you can utilize to help control your operations. These can be generated no matter what type of system you have:

- Output in terms of dollars per employee per day

- Actual hours applied to productive output compared with hours available for productive output

- Amount of overtime and in what areas

- Daily returns and credits

- Daily shipments

- Productivity compared with scheduled daily output by line

- Percentage of on-time shipments

- Daily rejects and reasons

- Daily raw materials purchases by item

- Percentage of machinery-utilization time used versus time available

- Dollar levels of inventories in raw form, work in process, and finished goods

- Daily sales

- Back-order position

- All accidents

- Variances of all types (labor, material, and overhead absorption) if you use standard costing

- Scrap and material disposition

- Field complaints

These are just a few of the reports that can be generated in addition to normal accounting reports (e.g., receivables aging, payables). In certain businesses, such as retail chains, activity and profitability per store are necessary to control operations.

The key to control is to utilize those reports that are meaningful to your business. Turnaround people zero in on the specific reports that are key indicators of the health of the business and follow those reports closely.

RESEARCH AND DEVELOPMENT

Research and development is like boat ownership: It is a hole in the budget into which one throws money and that may in the future yield some favorable results. The reality is that R&D is very much dependent on the type of company you are running and the type of market you are in. There are essentially three different approaches to products or service:

1. Be the leading-edge innovator.

2. Copy the idea but do it better.

3. Copy the idea but do it cheaper.

BE THE LEADING-EDGE INNOVATOR

If a company is an innovator and its business strategy is based on innovation, it is very difficult to modify that structure without seriously modifying its customer base and its approach to the market.

Being an innovator carries the ability to charge higher prices for the products developed, develop patent protection, and obtain exclusivity in certain markets. This approach also allows certain tax write-offs for research efforts. The downside is that there is risk and investment associated with R&D that may not result in a useable product or may not result in an income stream until sometime in the future.

Turnaround people may reduce R&D investment in order to milk the existing product line, but a company will pay for this by having fewer new products later. A better approach is to reexamine the projects in the hopper, determine earlier which ones will yield marketable products, and then terminate the ones that are less certain. Pharmaceutical companies as well as software development companies are continually facing these hard choices.

COPY THE IDEA BUT DO IT BETTER

This approach calls for more development and less research. It says, "I'm going to take an existing product and add features that make it better than anyone else's." The automotive business is continually doing this in its cars by adding bells and whistles. This effort extends the life cycle of models and designs. The risks are obviously lower than pure innovation and may even generate some R&D-like breakthroughs.

COPY THE IDEA BUT DO IT CHEAPER

In this approach, innovation is not even considered. Instead, development is focused on making the product at the lowest possible cost so that the product can capture market through low prices. There may be a substitution of lower-durability materials and an accompanying shorter product life.

In brief, your R&D strategy must match your overall corporate strategy or it will fail. In reality, most companies have a blend of the approaches.

CHOOSING YOUR INITIAL APPROACH

The genesis of the quartz-watch industry is a microcosm of these three approaches. The first developers of electronic watches charged tremendous prices for their unique new devices. Then new generations of quartz watches came along that used liquid crystal displays (LCDs) instead of light-emitting diode (LED) displays while incorporating day, date, and other functions. Today you can buy a full-function watch or clock for $5 and throw it away when it stops functioning.

As I stated, your R&D strategy is very much a part of your total market strategy. The question therefore is what you should do and what approach you should take. This is not a simple task. You must ask yourself the following questions:

- How do my customers perceive my company?

- How do I wish my company to be perceived?

- How much money do I wish to allocate to research?

- How much time do I have to develop new products?

- What kind of development skills do I have within my organization?

- Can I buy or license the technology I need?

THE LEADING-EDGE APPROACH

In a pure R&D-oriented company, funding is a key element of the strategy. The length of time from concept to development of the final product often takes years and generates large negative cash flows. In the pharmaceutical industry, the time to develop, test, and obtain approval for a new proprietary drug can take decades and cost tens of millions of dollars.

In the case of the electronic watch business, several other strategies have emerged as the industry has matured. These are:

- Branded high-end electronic watches that are sold as jewelry

- Enhanced electronic devices that contain MP3 players, altimeters, compasses, etc.

These are clearly examples of the product-enhancement approach.

In the software business there is a similar investment in time and effort to develop new programs, which may or may not lead to salable products. It is usually less than that in the drug business, but there is extensive use of cash prior to ever seeing income. Scary, isn't it? But the advantages are:

- Development of a new market

- Ability to charge premium prices for the product

- Exclusivity for 17 years if the product is patented

- Ability to license technology

- Some R&D tax benefits

There are companies that utilize the R&D approach every day and have become quite successful.

IMPROVING ON AN EXISTING PRODUCT

A more cautious approach in industry is to improve upon existing technology. This happens quite often in response to competitive pressure. Companies will add features to their existing products or incorporate features offered by others into their own products.

A company should be looking at the competition at all times and asking the question: What is my marketing advantage? By obtaining the competitor's product and examining its features, one can begin to develop ideas for improving products. This approach may lead to a totally original concept that you wish to incorporate as your own.

In the companies I've run, I've always purchased and analyzed my competitors' devices for comparison purposes. Adding features, improving physical appearance or compactness, or using stronger materials always develop a competitive edge. The cost of this approach is much less than pure R&D and does not usually yield as much return as a big "hit" in the R&D area, but the risks of working with proven technology are much less.

MAKING THE PRODUCT MORE CHEAPLY

There are many companies whose avowed philosophy is to take existing products and make them cheaper for mass markets. For example, the entire generic-drug market takes existing products whose patents protections have expired and develops alternate low-priced substitutes without the research and other entry costs of the "ethical" pharmaceutical companies.

Changes in construction materials and production methodologies are common in this approach. The disadvantage of this approach is that the eventual product usually sells at much lower prices with lower margins and usually is at the late stage of the product life cycle. The advantage is that by virtue of price, the product or service is accessible to much larger markets.

PICKING YOUR PRODUCT—INPUT SOURCES

No matter what your R&D philosophy, a major barrier to moving ahead is identifying the area where you should concentrate your efforts. Where should the inputs for new products or product modifications come from? How should you initially screen new products prior to starting to invest in their development?

My favorite tool is the product-development committee. It is a think-tank group that convenes at a remote location that is conducive to contemplative thought without distraction. I usually ask the following type of people to be part of the group (no more than ten):

- Two or three of our customers, usually people I respect

- Two or three people from our sales force

- Our R&D director

- Our marketing vice president

- Someone who is not in our industry but whose thinking I admire

- The president of the company

- A bright young person from middle management

After getting them to sign confidentiality agreements, we go to work. At these meetings we brainstorm for two to three days about what products we feel the industry needs and the priority in which they are needed.

During the meeting everyone has an equal voice and may express his or her opinions, no matter how far-fetched. In order to make the meeting more effective I ask each person to begin thinking about and writing down ideas and wish lists at least 30 days prior to the meeting.

The committee passes its output to the sales team and internal management for comment and reprioritization suggestions. New ideas may be added at this point. The final test is running the list past a select group of customers to obtain their input. There are other sources of input, of course, including:

- A survey of your sales force

- A survey of your customers

- A review of what your competition has done

- A general survey of industry literature to see what technology is emerging

I normally change the committee each year to get new ideas from fresh sources.

Okay. Now that you've got some ideas, how can you boil down your list to only those that have the greatest probability of economic success? The answer is to develop a preliminary business plan for each of the final ideas to determine the cost of development and the potential payback from its implementation.

The marketing department, with the assistance of R&D, engineering, and finance, now must come up with the business plan or projected development proposal. It should contain the following elements:

- The project description

- The estimated labor hours and costs to obtain a prototype or alpha version of the product

- The time to get to the prototype

- The cost of physically producing the prototype

- The estimated testing time

- The estimated tooling costs and time to obtain tooling

- The investment in machinery and equipment necessary to produce the product

- The estimated cost of the final product per unit

- A 10-year projection of sales, in both volume and dollars, reflecting expected sales prices

- Incremental support costs including commissions and administrative costs

- Eventual expected profitability and return on investment (ROI)

- Ancillary expected revenues, such as licenses

By now you're saying "Oh, Lord, if I did that I'd never get anything done." However, you are about to enter into one of the company's most costly areas of investment, and without a preliminary screen of development projects you are literally flying blind.

How many times have companies entered a project because someone in a senior position "just liked it" without fully investigating the ramifications of the decision? How many times have R&D teams developed devices for which there was no real market? The project screen minimizes risk and identifies those projects that will never pass the ROI test. The screen forces marketing, engineering, production, and finance to collaborate on and approve an R&D project.

There is one more step before starting a project besides obtaining funding, and that is to set up a project-tracking system to ensure that the project is "on time" and "on cost." There are off-the-shelf computer programs that aid in this regard and allow a weekly review of development on each project in which you are engaged.

If I have any scars on my back from business mistakes (I have many), the deepest is the one related to tracking R&D projects. Early in my career I was working as a supplier to a Fortune 100 company. Our company provided a key piece of equipment to this large and prestigious client. As a result of years of confidence-building relationships, the customer asked us to develop a piece of equipment for it that had enormous sales potential. I ran the concept past our management group and we developed a proposal that utilized unique technology from both the client company and our company. As part of the proposal, my R&D director set an 18-month time line to a working prototype. We developed and signed a contract for both the R&D phase and the product sales phase.

As part of my weekly management meetings I would ask my R&D director about progress. The response was always the same: "We are on target." I warned him of the dire consequences of not meeting the contractual delivery dates and told him if he identified problems early enough I could renegotiate the time lines. He assured me that he would let me know if we were in trouble, that I would have plenty of warning, and that I shouldn't worry. One week prior to the date we were to deliver the final product proto- type, he walked in and informed me that he needed another year to develop the technology.

He apparently had been feeding me false information and had told his people to "clam up" when I questioned them regarding progress. I won't even go into the subsequent pain and destruction of years of goodwill with our largest customer. I swore that I would never let that happen to me again and as a result I demand key milestones with any R&D project. I review all projects on a weekly basis to ensure that the timing and economics have not changed. My "bull" detector is very finely tuned.

Often a company can put a project back on track through the use of additional personnel or outside design services. But if the economics change unfavorably midway through the project, it may be best to terminate the project and save further investment instead of blindly moving ahead. This is an economic decision rather than an emotional one.

Another problem with R&D is that engineers like to hang on to the baby (the project) that they have been nurturing for many months. The time line forces the birth of the project at a given time. I have always had a problem with R&D wanting to "tweak" or "tune" the final product to the detriment of the schedule.

On a final note, suppose you have developed a brand-new product and are about to launch it. Be sure to patent those features that are unique and patentable. Many companies are loath to do this because of the cost of obtaining patents. This is a case of false economics. Besides providing a barrier to entry by others and a market advantage, a patent provides the opportunity for later li- censing of the development. Intellectual property also adds to the value of a company if it is ever sold. International patents are es- sential for those countries in which you plan to market and are cheaper and easier to obtain once the U.S. patent is approved.

CHAPTER SEVENTEEN

BANKING

How many times have you heard the expressions "my banker is my friend" or "I have a great relationship with my banker"? These may be true, but really your banker is a vendor who sells you money—a very important vendor but a vendor nevertheless.

One must understand that almost every turnaround involves renegotiating terms and conditions of the lending arrangement with a bank or other type of lender. These negotiations can be adversarial because I usually represent the debtor. On the other hand, if they are structured properly, there can be a win-win situation allowing the company the ability to survive and the bank the ability to recover its loan.

The turnaround lesson that can be utilized in your banking arrangements is that if your loan agreements are structured properly at the time the loan is consummated, then the probability of having problems in the future is vastly diminished.

TYPES OF BANK PROBLEMS

There are a number of events that may affect a bank and can have negative implications to a lender. Let's examine each in turn.

ECONOMIC CONDITIONS

The availability of loans and their interest rates are greatly influenced by general economic conditions at the time of the loan. If there is a great deal of liquidity in the marketplace and banks are competing for business, interest rates tend to be low and banks will take greater risks with potential clients. If the Federal Reserve tightens up the money supply, then loans are harder to get and rates are higher. Banks are subject to the laws of supply and demand, just like you are.

BANK MERGERS AND CONSOLIDATIONS

Over the last few years there have been numerous bank mergers, and as a result you may find yourself in the position of having a new parent bank that holds your loan. Your relationship with the bank may change due to a change in personnel. Even worse, the new bank may not like your loan or may decide to rid itself of companies in your industry even though you have not violated any conditions of the loan. This applies especially to industries that the lender may identify as high risk.

UNDERPERFORMANCE

If you have had "bumps" in your relationship with the bank, for example, a late payment or two or a minor covenant violation, the bank may classify your loan as "underperforming" and express a desire that you go elsewhere. An offshoot of this is that the bank may be forced to increase its loan loss reserves in anticipation of further problems.

REGULATION

The Federal Deposit Insurance Corporation (FDIC) and the Federal Reserve regulate banks. Even though your bank may consider your loan as performing, the regulations may not and may force the bank to reclassify your loan.

HIGHLY LEVERED TRANSACTIONS (HLTs)

The definition of an HLT can vary and depends on your debt-to-equity ratio. Your loan may become an HLT and be treated differently. Regulatory agencies normally mandate this definition.

CHANGING LEVELS OF SCRUTINY

Since the Enron and Tyco debacles, banks have more closely scrutinized loans and interpreted financial data more conservatively. Conservative interpretation by public accountants may also adversely change perceptions of a company's performance, which in turn may cause violations of loan covenants.

WHAT A BANK IS LOOKING FOR IN A LOAN

In most lending situations bankers are seeking several criteria prior to lending. The degree to which these criteria are satisfied will affect the conditions of the loan as well as the interest rate. The criteria are:

- **Viability of the Business.** This is determined by the historical track record of the business from a P&L standpoint and the business plan going forward.

- **Understandability of the Business Concept.** Bankers don't invest in businesses they don't understand and believe will not be in existence for the term of the loan. This includes considering the competitive environment of the business.

- **Equity.** Banks like equity investors who may be

prepared to step up with capital if the business gets in trouble, hence the desire for personal guarantees, which eventually force further equity contributions. The day of very highly leveraged transactions is essentially over due to regulatory constraints.

- **The Character of Management.** The honesty and character of the managers and owners are very important to a bank, as is stability in key positions.

- **The Collateral Available for the Loan.** Banks want to see sufficient collateral in terms of receivables, inventories, and machinery and equipment to recover their loans in the event of default. This is especially true of asset-based lenders (ABLs), which rely heavily on this security. Again, the personal guarantee provides another level of collateral to the lender.

- **Communication.** Last, the lender wants a schedule of reports and guaranteed communication with the company so he or she knows what's going on.

THE BANKING RELATIONSHIP AND HOW TO MANAGE IT

There are several keys to taking control of your banking relationship and optimizing the conditions under which you borrow money. They are:

- Get to know your banker and let him or her know the key personnel in the company (e.g., the chief financial officer).

- Regularly review the operations of your company and your business plan with your banker.

- *Never* lie to your banker.

- Keep your banker informed of both favorable and unfavorable events in the business—*no surprises*.

- *Always* have an alternative banking source available.

The last of these items is especially important. I stated at the beginning of this chapter that you should realize that your banker is a vendor like others. It would be foolish to have only one source for a key component of your product. Likewise it would be foolish to have a single potential lender. This means that the development of a relationship with a second bank does several things:

- It keeps your current lender honest and competitive with regard to rates and conditions of your loan.

- It gives you a place to go quickly if your current lending arrangement is compromised in any way.

- It gives you negotiating power.

The second bank relationship may involve occasional meetings with officers of the second institution or the presence of a minor account at the second bank. But all of us know what happens if you are forced to seek new lending in a short time frame. If you are lucky enough to find a secondary lender, the borrowing rates are significantly higher and the conditions of the loan are much more severe.

A key to managing your banking arrangement is the financial projections—what is normally called your budget. The budget document and its updates are the financial document that drives your relationship. Here's why:

- Your performance is measured against it.

- Your loan covenants are based on the numbers you project.

Most businesses have seasonal ups and downs, or if they are growing may have cash needs beyond that of a steady-state business. The projection you give the bank should be conservative in nature and reflect a less ebullient projection than those projections you use for the sales force or the board of directors. It should reflect your cash needs in a realistic manner and allow for contingencies. The penalties for breaking a covenant can be:

- A high fee for forbearing the incident, if it is a minor covenant

- An increase in the interest rate to what is called an upset rate (usually 2–3 points above the normal interest rate)

- Calling the loan (i.e., forcing immediate repayment) if the violation is severe enough

Each year, just as your bank reviews its relationship with your company, you should review your relationship with the bank by asking yourself the following questions:

- Is my lender meeting my company's needs in terms of services? This can include payroll services, clearing of deposits, letters of credit, clearing of checks, and resolution of disputes.

- Is my bank charging a competitive rate for my loans, or can I get better terms elsewhere?

- Does the bank have overly onerous conditions in the loan document?

- Can I get a loan elsewhere without a personal guarantee or with less collateral?

- How easy is my banker to work with, and can he meet my borrowing needs as the company grows?

Many companies stay in less-than-optimum loans because of "comfort" with the current lender. Again, you should review your relationship with your lender annually, especially if the company has had a very good year and as a result represents a lower level of risk to the bank.

LOAN DOCUMENTS—TAKING CONTROL

The lesson that all turnaround people know is that the loan documents and language in those documents will affect your total relationships with your lender. The more liberal your bank document, the easier it is to come to an equitable arrangement with the lender when things go awry.

Let's examine the types and elements of loan documents that you should be aware of:

Fixed-Term Loans—A loan for a fixed period of time with a specific payment schedule identified in the loan documents.

Revolver—A loan of a fixed maximum amount that may be drawn down at the discretion of the borrower and remains in place for a period of time determined by the loan documents.

Asset-Based Loan (ABL)—This loan relies on inventories, receivables, and other assets for its securitization. The loan size is normally a percentage of the value of the assets. This percentage is normally called "the advance rate." If lending is just against receivables, the common term used is "factoring."

The contractual conditions for most business loans vary. I go into detail here because each condition in a loan document can be negotiated depending on the strength of the company and competitive market conditions.

Rate—The interest rate charged by the lender can be fixed for the term of the loan or can vary according to some index such as the prime rate or the London Inter-Bank Offered Rate (LIBOR). This rate can be negotiated. Rates for excellent companies are sometimes below prime, but risky loans may carry rates as high as prime plus 4 or 5 percent. When a company has been doing well, it can sometimes go back to the lender and get a lower rate.

Term—The term or amortization period of the loan is also negotiable. Quite often, turnaround personnel reduce the cash strain on a company by renegotiating the term in order to extend out the principal payments or move some payments to the end of the loan (balloon). Also it is best not to have a prepayment penalty if the company wishes to extract itself from the loan early.

Advance Rate—In the ABL loan, a major negotiation relates to the advance rates that are offered against assets. For example, an 80 percent advance rate against receivables that are less than 60 days old is typical. You can negotiate this rate up to as much as 90 to 95 percent depending on the quality of the receivable. Certain receivables, such as government receivables, are typically disqualified (there are other lenders for government receivables). The same idea applies to inventories (typically 50–70 percent for finished goods, 70–80 percent for current raw material, and 0–10 percent for work in process) and plant and equipment. Each of these categories can be negotiated to optimum levels. The methods for valuing the inventory become very important as part of the negotiations as well.

Default Sections—This refers to the parts of the loan agreement that name the conditions the borrower must maintain in order to avoid a default. This can be a debt-to-equity ratio, a minimum cash requirement, a maximum negative cumulative cash flow, etc., plus the requirement for timely payment of interest and principle. If a company violates a covenant, it may be subject to a series of punishments. Another area of negotiation is the "cure period" to fix the problem. It is normally 30 to 60 days and is also negotiable. If a default occurs, the bank will usually charge an upset rate so that your woes multiply by having to pay even greater interest. The conditions of imposition of this rate plus the conditions for its removal are an important part of the loan document.

Right of Offset—Banks like to have the right of offset, which means if you default they can reduce your debt by seizing the cash in the accounts you have with the lender. This is a good reason to have small accounts at other lenders.

Deemed Insecure—This is an omnibus provision that allows the lender to terminate the loan if you are "deemed insecure." This means that if your industry begins to tank, even though you have met all your other contractual obligations, the bank can exit the loan with notice to the borrower. It's a back door for the bank to get out of a loan. The bank usually does this by informing you that it wishes you to pay off the loan within a given period of time (90–120 days) and wishes you to seek another source of funds. It may also begin dropping its advance rates on accounts receivable and inventory.

Fees—There are all sorts of additional fees that banks can and do charge for their services beyond interest. Audit fees, interest on the unused portion of the revolver, transaction fees, as well as legal fees are some of these. You can place limitations on or eliminate some of these fees in your negotiations.

Cross–Collateralization/Cross–Defaults—Often the bank gains additional security in a loan by asking for cross-collateralization or cross-defaults against other companies or assets owned by the parent company. Nonpayment or default on a different corporate loan can trigger a default on the one you are seeking. This obviously should be avoided.

Change of Control—Most loans carry a change-of-control provision that allows a bank to force immediate repayment of the loan if more than 50 percent, or a number to be negotiated, of the ownership changes and key operating personnel change. If the provision is broad enough, this is seldom a problem, except at the time of a sale.

It's important to obtain a really good attorney to assist in the drafting of loan documents to ensure that your interests are served. Many small-company borrowers are blissfully unaware of what they are agreeing to.

THE PERSONAL GUARANTEE

The biggest problem for privately held or closely held companies is the personal guarantee. The personal guarantee usually guarantees all the assets of the owners or senior managers of a company as security for a loan. These types of guarantees are problematic for a turnaround person because they add the burden for repayment of the loan to the individual as well as the company. The temptation to get out of the loan by declaring bankruptcy is diminished by the fact that personal bankruptcy also has to occur.

Unfortunately, many loans to medium or small companies require personal guarantees. Here are some rules regarding pledging personal assets:

- Avoid them if you can trade other concessions such as rate or term in place of a personal guarantee.

- Limit the amount of the personal guarantee to a

specific amount you can afford. It may represent only a portion of your assets.

- Set conditions for the personal guarantee to be reduced or eliminated based on the performance of the loan. For example, if the company meets its budgeted profit goals for three years in a row, the guarantee is eliminated or the guarantee is reduced by one fifth for each year the loan is in place.

- Identify specific personal assets that back the guarantee and allow substitution of new assets for old.

Lenders will want your spouse to sign a personal guarantee since most states have joint-ownership laws. Try to avoid this as well.

OTHER LENDERS OR SOURCES OF MONEY

There are an almost infinite variety of ways to obtain cash for running a business. Turnaround experts are trained to seek the best of these alternatives for their clients, while keeping in mind that the lowest-price loan or source may not be the best answer depending on the loan conditions described in this chapter. Some of these alternative sources are:

ABL Lenders—They do not rely on the traditional performance of the company but rather the salability of its assets.

Bonds and Commercial Paper—Issuing bonds as a method of raising cash is a form of borrowing from the general public. Smaller companies often use bonds to raise funds for real estate purchases (industrial development revenue bonds) for factories and other facilities.

Venture Capital and Private Equity Funds—There are venture capital companies or private equity funds that will provide cash in return for equity or will lend money. They often have the expectation of "cashing out" in three to five years. Usually these funds want control (over 50 percent) of the business when they make equity investments.

Private Investors—This is similar to venture capital but represents fewer investors, either as a loan, an equity infusion, or both.

Suppliers—Often good suppliers provide funding if they wish to own part of the business or are willing to make loans to the company.

Government Sources—There are a variety of government entities that provide loans or grants to companies, such as the Small Business Administration (SBA).

Secondary Lenders—There are lenders that specialize in specific industries, in distressed companies, or other specific categories. The interest rates on loans from these specialty commercial lenders tend to be much higher than on loans from commercial banks.

THE WORKOUT

The last area of advice I wish to offer in dealing with lenders is what to do if your loan is in duress. You may have violated covenants or missed payments. The lender will have sent in a team to discuss the situation and sent a formal default letter to start the clock on the cure period. The company may find itself dealing with the "special assets" section of the bank if it has an underperforming loan.

The answer to all these events is to get help immediately. No company is normally equipped to handle this situation. You will need a very good lawyer plus a turnaround crisis manager to act on your behalf. There tend to be emotional issues as well as economic issues in tackling this problem, and it is best to use third parties that will negotiate on your behalf. Often companies try this themselves. It is a grave and often fatal mistake.

Finally, suppose the workout is successful and the company is able to recover from its problems. It is then time to get another bank or lender, because your original bank relationship is spoiled. The memories of the company's failure to perform properly will linger, so it is better to start afresh with a new lender.

CHAPTER EIGHTEEN

FRAUD

Fraud in a company works just like high blood pressure in a human being. It is not obvious and eventually kills if it is not detected and cured. It is estimated that fraud played a major part in over 50 percent of the business failures in the United States over the last decade.

In most of the businesses I have helped over the last 30 years, I have always found fraud and theft in varying degrees. The Enron and Tyco failures pointed out that there can be an atmosphere of fraudulent conduct that extends from top management down into the rank and file of a corporation. In the Enron failure, not only was the public defrauded, but many innocent Enron employees lost their life savings.

The subject that I will discuss in this chapter relates to internal theft, which destroys the company from within, and what to do about it. There are types of theft that employees and most employers do not consider theft, yet represent a taking of the company's resources. The largest of these is the theft of time. This is usually in the form of extended personal phone calls, the use of the Internet at the office for nonbusiness purposes, or the personal use of office supplies and other office items.

CONDITIONS THAT LEAD TO THEFT

This first section deals with real, premeditated, outright fraud, either to enhance one's own position within the company or to line one's pockets. Here are some situations that create breeding grounds for theft.

LACK OF ADEQUATE CONTROL

The failure to put adequate controls in place can encourage theft. In a mining company I was involved with, the miners were paid based on output. They would truck the product to a scale and weigh it before taking the ore to a site where it would be dumped to await refining. The scale would produce a ticket, and incentive pay was generated based on the month's tickets. The only problem was that the tickets were not date stamped or time stamped, and the trucker was not identified. You guessed it. The miners and truckers were in cahoots and would run the truck back over the scale an extra couple of times a shift. When it came time to inventory the ore, the company was missing a mountain of ore. We ended up firing all the miners and truckers and starting with a new crew.

I'm not saying that you need to track everything, but one must be intelligent about obvious gaps in control.

WHERE THERE ARE DRUGS, THERE IS THEFT

In one company, I discovered huge, unaccounted inventory losses. Scrap and miscounting could not account for the levels we were seeing. In our investigations we found that drugs were being sold out of the food-vendor truck that came by the plant each shift (commonly called "the roach coach"). When we had the vendor arrested by the police our shrinkage began to diminish, and when I put in a mandatory drug-testing program we got rid of the thieves. Obviously, drug habits have to be fed and the easiest way to cover such a habit is by stealing from the company.

RELIANCE ON YOUR AUDITORS
TO DISCOVER THEFT

Normal auditors are not equipped to discover theft. Their engagement letters these days attest to the fact that they are not able to do so. One of the worst cases of internal theft on multiple levels was at a company that had just passed an audit with flying colors. A forensic accounting firm can identify possible areas of theft; however, a forensic audit is quite costly.

IF THE NUMBERS DON'T LOOK RIGHT,
THEY USUALLY AREN'T

In those instances where I've been able to detect fraud, I have found something wrong with the numbers.

For example, I once had a remote plant operation that would provide its daily operations data through a computer download. I was reviewing overtime numbers and discovered that our payroll clerk was working a great deal of overtime. I then called the plant manager to chastise him for working her so hard because she was nearing retirement. His response was that he, in fact, had her on shortened hours and couldn't understand the overtime. An investigation showed that she had been falsifying her hours for months and had done it for a number of others in the plant. We had her arrested and marched through the plant.

In another instance I noticed that the cost of plant consumables was rising at 10 percent per year while sales had been dropping at 5 percent per year and inflation was only at 1 or 2 percent per year. I called the purchasing agent who handled plant consumables, which were $20 million per year, and asked him about the apparent disparity in numbers. He vowed that inflation was the problem and that my estimate of 1 to 2 percent did not apply to those items he purchased. A subsequent investigation by a professional exposed the fact that he was taking kickbacks from suppliers to the tune of over $1 million a year.

IF SOMETHING DOESN'T MAKE SENSE, THERE'S SOMETHING WRONG

In one company, I was touring a division that made a very high-tech, high-specification product for the U.S. Navy. It was made under clean-room conditions utilizing specialized computer-based machinery. I asked the president of the division if we had any competition, and he indicated there was another company that bid against us and won one out of three bids. I said I was surprised that any other company would invest as much as we did in such a limited market. His feeling was that the other company didn't but that it instead manufactured the product using low-overhead methods.

Since the production was dependent on technology to achieve the tolerance required by the Navy, I said that his premise had to be incorrect. He mentioned that the competitor's plant was around 10 miles away and we could see it from the road if we wanted to drive there. We did exactly that and discovered two Quonset huts in a dusty field. I immediately returned to the plant and phoned some ex-CIA investigators. We placed a mole in the plant, working as a janitor. Within 48 hours we had our answer. Our entire third shift was making the product for our competitor. Our foreman was burying the materials losses in our sizable scrap rates. He was transporting the product past our gate guards in the trunk of his car. We prosecuted and put the other company out of business.

I have seen the theft of both very large and very small items. I have had a chief financial officer steal from petty cash to support a drug habit. I have seen a CEO and CFO create a slush fund out of which they paid themselves extraordinary bonuses.

WHAT TO DO IF YOU SUSPECT FRAUD

Here are some tips for dealing with suspected fraud:

- **Use professionals to investigate.** Don't try to do it internally. The use of investigators and forensic accountants will give you real data without compromising any results that may have to be used in court.

- **Set up a system for good employees to report misbehavior or theft anonymously.** A special phone number or place to report without recrimination is a way to detect fraud. I would rather a whistle-blower report a problem internally so that a company can police its own problems.

- **Close obvious security gaps.** The use of closed-circuit TV and other security equipment can deter theft.

- **Allow access to secure areas only to those who need to be there.** Badge control keeps the wrong people out of the wrong spaces.

- **Do background checks on all personnel who handle money.** Alert personnel in the company to be diligent to anything strange going on and to report it immediately.

CHAPTER NINETEEN

BANKRUPTCY AS A TOOL

No one likes to consider the alternative of bankruptcy, but in some instances it provides the only means of ensuring the survival of a company and the jobs and economic entity that it represents. It can also be used to "clean up" a messy legal structure in anticipation of a sale or an acquisition.

This chapter discusses Chapter 11 of the bankruptcy code and only refers to corporate reorganization. I am not an attorney, and if you are contemplating bankruptcy, you will need the best bankruptcy counsel that you can get to act on your behalf. However, I have acted as chief restructuring officer (CRO) in a number of bankruptcies and have operated companies through the complexity of the bankruptcy process and emerged successfully from bankruptcy.

Realize that bankruptcy can be an expensive process because the debtor pays for all the attorneys and advisers in a case. There are reasons to utilize the bankruptcy process and it is worth mentioning as an alternative.

POSSIBLE REASONS FOR
CHAPTER 11 DECLARATIONS

There are a number of possible reasons to declare bankruptcy under Chapter 11 of the bankruptcy code. These are:

- Insolvency or anticipated insolvency.

- To give the company the ability to get a "breather" and make settlements with its creditors.

- Pressure from secured lenders.

- Legal action by others, which might make the company insolvent.

- Legacy payments such as unfunded pension plans whose mandatory payments would leave the company insolvent.

- Executory contracts such as leases or other contracts that are causing the company distress.

- A desire to "clean up" old potential legal obligations prior to the eventual sale of the company or its assets. A potential purchaser may also desire this.

If a company is in financial trouble, the bankruptcy code allows the company to take a "breather" by this declaration. At one time bankruptcy carried a terrible stigma, very few companies emerged from it because their sales dried up, and the companies died from lack of revenues. In fact, the public has become so used to bankruptcy that some companies have thrived under bankruptcy and have emerged as even stronger entities. Virtually every one of the major airlines has been in or is in bankruptcy. A number of retail chains have also gone through Chapter 11 with no adverse effects on the businesses' sales.

BANKRUPTCY PROCESS

I would like to discuss the process in nonlegal terms so that you can understand the course one can take under a bankruptcy scenario.

First of all, a declaration of bankruptcy usually gives current management "debtor-in-possession" (DIP) status unless there is a question as to the debtor's honesty or ability to run the company (in which case the court may appoint a trustee). It is rare in Chapter 11 cases that a trustee actually runs the company. The court usually names a U.S. trustee to interact with management and others to ensure that everyone follows the process correctly.

DEBT

The declaration of bankruptcy mandates that the debtor cannot pay any of its unsecured debt, such as accounts payable, unless authorized by the court; thus, the demands for payment by vendors are abated. Purchases of new items such as raw materials, supplies, and other essential items necessary to do business, including salaries and insurance, can be made upon approval of the court.

Thus, there is a tremendous cash relief to the company due to the "stay" of old debts. Vendors can continue to sell to the company and any new debts incurred get "superpriority" status in terms of eventual repayment.

There is an absolute "pecking order" with regard to how debts will get paid according the reorganization plan. First are administrative claims and superpriority claims, then secured debt, then unsecured debt, and finally equity. The arrangement with each of these creditors is made in a court-approved "plan" that essentially determines when everybody will be paid, how much, and in what form. The "plan" is usually formulated by the company and is approved by the creditors who carry weight, dependent upon their "class" (secured or nonsecured) and the amount they are owed.

Others may offer a competing plan, but the company (debtor in possession) has an exclusive period of time in which to propose the plan.

The company needs money to operate while in bankruptcy, so it obtains debtor-in-possession financing, usually from its current bank. This financing is another superpriority item and usually carries hefty interest rates.

Besides the mandated stay as to payment of debt, the company receives a very important power: the power to accept or reject "executory" contracts. Now, the nature of an executory contract is extremely broad. Here are a few examples:

- Leases on property

- Employment contracts

- Union contracts

- Licenses received or given

- Leases on equipment and vehicles

- Pension plans

- Purchase and sales agreements

It doesn't take a genius to figure out that this ability to reject or accept agreements can save a company an immense amount of money. Retailers who are in bad mall leases can reject those leases. If your company is in an onerous delivery contract with a vendor, this provision allows you to reject it. Rejection of an agreement also gives the rejected party the ability to file an unsecured claim for the extent to which it has been damaged.

This provision sets the stage for a company to negotiate concessions prior to bankruptcy. In a company in which I was involved, we had a large number of cellular towers on various parcels of leased land. A number of these were economically untenable due to the large rent payments. We therefore decided to renegotiate 4,000 leases prior to filing bankruptcy. We indicated that we would accept or reject the lease dependent on the results of the negotiation.

The result was a $2,000,000 annual savings in rent, which flowed directly to operating profit. In the event of acceptance of a lease, the lessor must be made whole through negotiations as to past unpaid rent and the lessor must be paid in a timely manner.

CONTRACTS

A great many contracts have bankruptcy provisions that state that the contract is null and void if either party declares bankruptcy. These provisions are generally useless under the law. If you as the bankrupt entity choose to accept a contract, the other party has no choice but to continue doing business for the term of the agreement, assuming it is not voided by nonpayment in the future.

I once ran a company that had licenses for intellectual property in the form of an agreement to manufacture a particular brand of clothing. The company was in bankruptcy, and we affirmed the license with the licensor. Despite the licensor's best efforts, it could not force us to stop using its brand name.

Bankruptcy also allows a company to eliminate management contracts that are not affordable under the prevalent economic situation. New arrangements are normally made with the court's approval for retention of management, and certain more afford-able retention incentives are put in place.

UNIONS

There is a special section in the code for dealing with union contracts, but in essence companies can utilize bankruptcy to reopen negotiations with a union. This might achieve savings or work conditions that will enhance the viability of the company. If the union refuses to negotiate, the court can, if it chooses to do so, enforce the proposed new terms.

Again, the mere threat of bankruptcy can cause a union to renegotiate or provide temporary economic relief to a company. I have often elicited the help of unions in turnarounds because the viability of the union is tied to the viability of the company. The airlines have learned this and have renegotiated contracts with their pilots, flight attendants, and ground personnel.

UTILITIES

Utilities, because of their unique monopolistic position, cannot deny service to a bankrupt company, but they can ask for and receive deposits that will make them secure.

LEGACY PAYMENTS

A big area of potential savings to a company is the ability to cancel or moderate what are called legacy payments.

A company may have a mandatory contribution pension plan that is untenable. The company can petition the court to terminate the plan. There are also many plans in the United States that are underfunded. The Pension Benefit Guarantee Corporation (PBGC) controls the rate at which these deficient funds are "made up" by companies. In bankruptcy, the PBGC acts on behalf of the pension fund and negotiates terms for repayment of the owed amounts. Pension funds are one of the legacy payments that Chapter 11 can mitigate. In some instances the PBGC must assume the obligation for the pension (within certain monetary limits). Arrangements with retirees are also covered under the laws and can be renegotiated with a committee of their representatives.

LEGAL SETTLEMENTS

Some companies will seek bankruptcy protection in anticipation of legal action that will render them insolvent. Usually this is done before a cash award is made because once an award is made it must be paid before unsecured claims in the eventual distribution scheme. Even if the court makes an award, bankruptcy limits the amount paid to that which is settled on in the plan.

BANKRUPTCY PLAN

All of the considerations covered above can be wrapped up in a "plan" that the debtor in possession has an exclusive right to present within a given set period of time. The plan spells out what each class of creditor gets, in what form, and over what period of time. It should satisfy the cash need of the company by stretching out the company's payments or compromising the old debt of certain classes of creditors. For example, the unsecured creditor may get 10 percent of what is owed in cash plus warrants to purchase new stock at a given price or a long-term payout of 50 percent of what is owed at no interest.

The variety of arrangements is infinite. The various classes vote on the plan, and if it is accepted, the company emerges from bankruptcy.

BENEFITS OF BANKRUPTCY

Obviously, I've omitted a lot but I wanted to illustrate that a company can achieve a lot through bankruptcy.

In one company I operated, the new financing (DIP) was provided by an equity holder (an investment firm). Upon emergence from bankruptcy, it converted its DIP financing, which had a priority position, into new equity in the company and ended up owning the company again. The company had been fixed by all the things we had done while under court protection, and the investment firm ended up with a brand-new viable entity.

Through the bankruptcy process, there is also a provision for selling the assets of a company to another company or for selling the company itself to another. This process has been utilized to clean up distressed companies and essentially start over.

I also want to discuss the prepackaged bankruptcy. When a company emerges from bankruptcy, it is considered a new company that is essentially free of the liabilities of the past. The prepackaged concept is to prearrange payment to all the constituencies, the secured lender, the creditors, etc., usually dollar for dollar. The company goes through a cleansing of potential warranty obligations, potential lawsuits, and other potential unrealized liabilities, so that it is "clean" for a sale. The bankruptcy is quick (60 days or less), and the plan is present before formally entering bankruptcy. This is usually done in anticipation of a sale.

DISADVANTAGES OF BANKRUPTCY

Now that I've described briefly the potential power of Chapter 11, I would like to discuss the downsides of bankruptcy:

- **Bankruptcy is costly.** It can cost a minimum of $100,000 up to many millions of dollars. The cost must be compared with the potential result. If the bankruptcy is successful, the cost is one of the burdens of the corporation.

- **Management doesn't have total control.** The debtor in possession doesn't entirely control the company's fate because the court must approve everything that is done.

- **It takes time.** There is a huge amount of negotiation

that must take place with many parties, each having their own agenda. The debtor doesn't always win what it wants.

■ **It's risky.** The process can go awry at a number of points, and the company can fail to meet its obligations and be forced into Chapter 7 liquidation.

In summary, bankruptcy is a powerful tool that must be used judiciously. It should be entered when there is enough money in the till to help carry the financial burden and pay for expert help in the form of excellent counsel and advisers.

CASHING OUT

Now that you've done all sorts of wonderful things to improve your business profitability, it is time to reap your rewards. The decision point with regard to selling all or part of an individual position in a company is primarily a function of two things:

1. The seller's desire to move cash into a personal estate and to try a new and fresh endeavor

2. The desire to improve the condition of the business from profitability and growth-potential standpoints

Obviously, the optimum time to cash out is when the business is doing well, has prospects for continued growth, and the owner has a desire to cash out, move on, or retire. An interim position would be a merger with a combination of a partial cash-out and your continued participation in the business. I always ask private owners or major stockholders to evaluate their personal plans after the cash-out to determine if they are truly ready to sell the company.

I have been on the board of or run numerous companies where the eventual goal has been to sell out, resulting in a payday for the investors in the company. The methodologies differ depending on the size and structure of the company. In each of the cases I am going to describe, I strongly recommend that you get assistance in the sale process unless the business is extremely small, and even then I would recommend that you get assistance in the sale process. I also recommend using a good attorney who has experience in the sale of businesses.

For anything larger, I would recommend a business broker or investment banker as well as an attorney to assist in the sale process. In fact, larger companies may wish to employ an internal consultant such as myself to help management through a time-consuming and potentially traumatic process. The reasons for enlisting help are:

- Owners and management teams tend to become emotionally involved in their businesses and have a hard time understanding the true value of the business.

- Most companies go through the sale process seldom in their lifetime, so they don't know the proper things to do.

- A sale process can be destructive to company morale if not handled properly.

- Confidentiality is usually important in a sale process, and a professional knows how to handle this aspect of a sale from a legal and an operational standpoint.

- If handled improperly, a potential sale can cause disruption in the revenue stream of the company being sold and give competitors an undeserved advantage.

- The preparation of the sales document is best left in the hands of professionals who know what to include and how to present such documents.

- During the sale process, the business must continue to operate and maintain its profitability. Hiring professionals helps remove part of the preparation burden from management's shoulders.

- Identification of the universe of potential buyers, both strategic and financial, domestic and international, is best left to people who have the contacts and know whom to call.

- Last but not least, there are a variety of legal issues connected to the sale, which, if not treated in the proper manner, can cause lawsuits and legal problems after the sale. I will discuss fraudulent conveyance later in this chapter.

Now that I've convinced you to get the proper assistance in your sale, let's examine the types of exit strategies that may be available to a company.

SMALL COMPANIES

Privately held companies smaller than $5 million in revenue that are sole proprietorships or small partnerships should use a business broker. These are individuals who are versed in selling companies who know the ins and outs of the legal process and are able to help an owner identify potential prospects for a sale. They work for and are paid by the seller. They give advice prior to the sale as to how to "dress up" the business in order to achieve the maximum value of the business. Many brokers are specialists in buying specific types of businesses.

For example, I know a restaurant broker extremely well in New York City. She knows the pulse of the business, she knows who all the players are, and she knows who may be interested in expanding a small chain or who may be selling. She knows all the major chefs and what they are planning to do, and she is a great resource in this specific genre.

Another important feature of utilizing brokers is that they can help with developing a true profit and loss statement for the company. What do I mean by this? Most small businesses or proprietorships tend to operate on a tax-minimization strategy; that is, the owners take aggressive stands on depreciation of assets, loss reserves, and other items that decrease taxable income. They may also have the business pay for items such as large life insurance policies, generous health plans, and other costs and ownership "perks" that are beyond those needed for the business. Management may also inflate its own salaries as a method of getting cash out of the business just as management may minimize its salaries during tough years to keep cash in the business.

The broker's job, along with a financial adviser, is to recast the financials to reflect what is normal in the business so that the P&L is optimized. The adjustments that are made are identified fully to the potential buyer so that there can be no question as to disclosure. This process usually provides a net income that is much higher than that shown on monthly or quarterly financials, and certainly on tax filings.

In privately or closely held corporations, I have seen the common practice of owning the real estate separately from the corporation and then charging rent at above-market rates to the corporation. This drives the corporation's income down while providing private ownership with both the depreciation and income from the real estate. It is just another way to move cash to the owners.

Another consideration for small companies is the tax consequences of the sale. Often sales can be structured to reduce the tax effects significantly for the seller. I advise sellers to employ the best tax adviser they can find prior to the sale process so that the sale can be structured to minimize federal, state, and local taxes. Fortunately, the long-term capital gains tax situation provides a lesser tax rate for most sellers.

The sale of assets may be better for the seller, or selling the company as a whole may be the best way to go. The company must make this decision before the company is offered for sale.

In smaller businesses there is always the option of selling to employees or to members of the family. In this case I would still pay a broker to provide a fair valuation of the business and would utilize an attorney to ensure that the sale is conducted properly. I would also structure long-term payouts and recourses if needed.

MEDIUM-SIZE COMPANIES—PRIVATELY OR CLOSELY HELD

In the sale of a medium-size company, you will probably need an investment banker. There are a wide variety of investment banks that can perform the sale function. I feel strongly that the investment bank should match the needs and size criteria of the company being sold. In other words, I most likely wouldn't recommend a huge investment bank to a midsize seller. Even though large investment banks have excellent resources, they pay the most attention to their high-potential-fee cases rather than smaller clients that they know will not generate large fees. Investment bankers charge fees based on the realized sales price, so the larger the company, the higher the potential fee.

I have a not-so-funny story in this regard. I was placed as CEO of a company that was going to be sold since the investor (an equity fund) wished to cash out. We decided to utilize one of the biggest investment banks in the United States in order to reach the widest group of potential purchasers and perhaps get an auction going to drive up the price. The expected price for the company was slightly over $100 million, which today is a medium to small deal. The managing partner of the equity fund and I met with the investment banking firm's senior partner, whom we both knew and trusted personally, and arranged for his company to handle the transaction. He assured us that he was going to be involved all the way to the final sale. As the preparations for the sale proceeded, I noticed that the people visiting the firm were becoming younger and less and less experienced. Finally one day as we were making presentations to a potential purchaser, I turned to the representative of the investment banking firm—who at this point looked like a high school student—and asked a technical question about the sale. He was unable to answer the question. I then asked how long he had been with the firm and it turned out that he was a summer intern.

At this point I exploded and asked that the senior partner of the investment banking firm call me immediately. I informed him that for the $5 million fee they were expected to get, I expected much better service. I demanded that he get his posterior on a plane and be in my office in the morning to discuss our arrangement. Needless to say, he showed up the next day for a very serious conversation.

The point of all this is that the investment bank must be chosen carefully to match the needs of the company. I prefer medium-size investment banks to which the seller is an important client. A good investment bank can perform the following functions for a company:

- It can structure the selling document ("the book") with the aid of management, so that it honestly shows the company in the best possible light without distorting or misrepresenting what is for sale.

- It can develop and control expectations as to the selling price that can reasonably be expected for the company as compared with sales of similar types of companies in similar markets.

- It can help identify onetime events, both positive and negative, that distort the company's financial statements and provide normalized statements for examination. Examples of this are onetime lawsuit settlements or business interruptions that are never expected to happen again. Windfall gains in income also fall into this category. If the business is privately held, the same normalization process can be used to discount unusual bonuses or other distributions.

- It can test management's projections of financial performance for reasonableness and consistency.

- It can help keep the process confidential by controlling the "book" and demanding confidentiality through nondisclosure agreements and internal limitations as to involvement in the sale process.

- It can suggest management incentives to keep key players involved in the process.

- It can, with management's help, identify key strategic players who are qualified to purchase the company and who may be interested and approach them on a confidential basis. A strategic buyer by definition is one who is already in the same business or a related business and for whom a strategic purchase would yield synergism beyond that found in a strictly financial purchase. Strategic buyers in most instances will pay more for a company than pure financial buyers.

- It can identify key financial buyers who may be interested in the seller's company and have the ability to obtain the cash to conduct the purchase. These buyers may be domestic or international.

- It will schedule and help management make presentations to potential buyers with regard to the company.

- If possible, it will encourage an auction among potential buyers to "bid up" the selling price and obtain a premium price for the company.

- It will coordinate the proper legal documents necessary for the sale and protect the client and the seller with regard to pre- and post-closing events such as representations and warranties in the sale.

Obviously a good lawyer who specializes in this area is needed. An excellent tax adviser is also needed.

Earlier I mentioned fraudulent conveyance, and because I

have been involved in several instances as the plaintiff in fraudulent conveyance cases, I thought it best to discuss at this point. Bluntly, fraudulent conveyance occurs when the purchaser feels that the seller has intentionally misrepresented what is being sold either through written documents and projections provided or through oral representations by key personnel. Even though the "book" has a disclaimer in the front that places the responsibility for verification of the information squarely back on the buyer, if there is an obvious attempt to deceive or defraud the buyer, the buyer may have a cause of action in the courts. A lawsuit of this type is usually lengthy and expensive but can result in a rescinded sale or a cash award to the buyer.

There are other ways one can cash out in a midsize company. These include using an employee stock-option plan (ESOP) or taking the company public through an initial public offering (IPO) and converting ownership into cash through the sale of stock.

THE ESOP

In the ESOP, the owners essentially provide the employees with the ability to purchase ownership in the company through options granted to the employees at a fixed price at a given time. This requires valuation of the company each time that the options are granted so that the options are at a fair price. This valuation must be done by an independent third party. There must be a certain amount of disclosure to the employees as to the condition of the company so that they are fully informed buyers of the stock. This is a lengthy process, and the conversion of the ownership's interest into cash takes place as the employees exercise their options. There are tax advantages to this form of conversion, but an expert should be consulted before embarking down this path of ownership. Over time the control shifts entirely to the employees.

Because I have never done an ESOP, I mention it here as a point of interest and a possible option to be investigated as one path to liquidity.

THE IPO

Another method of cashing out is to take a company public by offering stock for sale to the general public. The process is somewhat similar to selling to another company except that the buyers use one of the stock exchanges to purchase the shares. In order to conduct an IPO, one must first find a licensed brokerage or dealership firm that is willing to act as a lead underwriter of the offering. It in turn will help write the equivalent of the "book" in a private sale, which is called a "red herring."

The red herring is a disclosure statement that describes in detail the business, its competitors, its market, its financial performance, its key personnel, etc. The Securities and Exchange Commission dictates what must be disclosed in this document and reviews the document for content and accuracy. Fraudulent or misleading statements in the red herring can lead to fines and/or criminal proceedings against the company and its officers.

The underwriter may syndicate the offering with other brokerage firms depending on its size and desirability. The underwriter usually asks management to help in the sale of the stock by presenting the offering to analysts and brokers through what is affectionately called a "road show." Presuming all goes well, the offering is then sold to the public.

ADVANTAGES OF A PUBLIC OFFERING

Public offerings come with some upsides, such as the following:

- Owners can maintain control of a company while selling off part of their ownership.

- The multiple of earnings at which a stock is traded can be much higher than that realized through the private sale of a company and can return much more to ownership.

- Ownership or management can sell its remaining interest in a company (subject to SEC and market restrictions) at a later time as the company grows and gains value.

- Stock options can be offered as incentives to key personnel.

DISADVANTAGES OF A PUBLIC OFFERING

Public offerings also come with some downsides, such as the following:

- The company now comes under the scrutiny of the SEC and its strict financial reporting rules.

- It must disclose all major events that affect performance.

- It must conduct mandated audits with strict reporting requirements.

- It must allow all shareholders to vote on a number of issues including the board of directors.

- Key personnel must report when they plan to sell stock and are unable to sell stock during certain periods of time.

- Ownership and management usually cannot trade their stock for a limited period of time.

With the advent of Sarbanes-Oxley and other legislation, some public companies have considered going private in order to mitigate the costly audit and reporting requirements of public companies. Also, the possible exposure of officers and boards of directors to prosecution and fines as a result of perceived fraud have made IPOs less appealing.

THE LARGE PRIVATE COMPANY AND
ALL PUBLIC COMPANIES

Again, the investment bank is a must in the sale of large private and all public companies. The large-company private sale is no different from the medium-company sale except that the importance of the investment bank's contacts and the level of those contacts is accentuated. The ability of the investment bank to call and reach the topmost levels of the target buyer is possibly a key to the sale.

In a public-company environment, special attention must be paid to the public-announcement aspects of the transaction where a sale or merger enhances the value of the stock. If a company announces that it will entertain offers for its stock, it must form a special committee of the board to evaluate any offers received. Each offer is evaluated to determine if it adequately represents the true value of the company regardless of the traded price of the stock. A valuation expert is also used in these instances to guide the special committee in its recommendation to the shareholders. A shareholder vote is the final determinant if the company is to be sold. However, the government must approve the sale as well to ensure that the merger does not create a monopoly or other restraint of trade.

GOLDEN RULES OF CASHING OUT

I have been involved in many sales and mergers of companies both public and private and several rules hold true:

- They always take longer than expected.

- They always cost more time and money than expected.

- If not organized like a military drill, they are absolute chaos.

- Something emerges that neither side expected.

CHAPTER TWENTY-ONE

THE BOARD

I feel that every company, no matter the size, should have a board of advisers or directors. Of course, corporations are required to have a board of directors, and public companies must have boards of directors with outside directors. A board of advisers is not the same as a board of directors, but the ability and necessity of a CEO to stand up each quarter in front of individuals who may question his or her actions is important in keeping management sharp. This prevents management from becoming too insular and inwardly directed, and it helps prevent the CEO from making strategic errors.

If the boards are properly composed, it brings fresh ideas to the company and cuts through internal arrogance. It provides a sounding board for ideas and concepts and brings other points of view and the wisdom of experience to the table.

CHOOSING A BOARD

Too often a board consists of pals of the CEO who will endorse any idea he or she brings forth, providing little more than a rubber stamp to the actions of a company. A really good board is made up of people who have been successful at what they do and are willing to express their opinions based on their knowledge or experience.

Several members of the board should work for the company; they provide specific input and coordinate board actions. These members are typically the president or CEO and the company's chief financial officer. Other staff personnel can be invited to board meetings but should not be members.

OUTSIDE MEMBERS

Here are some thoughts on the characteristics of nonmanagement board members:

- **They should be in related but not competitive businesses.** The idea of having someone in a related business as part of the board is twofold: It brings additional knowledge of the business to the board and it may bring ideas about trends, emerging problems, and opportunities to the board. Nonmanagement board members might be people who provide ancillary services such as distribution or manufacturing in your space. They can also identify sales opportunities within your space.

- **They should be people whose business acumen you admire.** Adding successful businesspeople whose wisdom and knowledge you admire and who are willing to offer opinions adds greatly to the board mix. They should have operated other companies as CEOs and understand the problems of someone sitting in that role.

- **They should be people who are leaders in their field and have the specific knowledge to enhance**

the company's operations. Their technical knowledge or expertise can provide key guidance to the company. Good candidates include academics who are involved in your field or industry specialists.

- **They should be involved parties.** I have usually sat on the boards of companies owned by equity funds. One or two of their representatives should be on the board. I have found that keeping the investors informed and close at hand helps immensely in moving a company forward.

- **They should be sales or marketing specialists or people strong in your weak areas.** I find that one of my soft spots is sales and marketing. I always fill board spots in areas where I feel that I am weaker than others to provide sage advice.

THE BOARD MEETING

I have attended the board meetings of large private companies that have extremely loose, unwritten agendas. The end result was like Brownian movement—we bounced back and forth among subjects without real direction and made no real decisions. We often forgot important items. So here are my thoughts on running effective board meetings.

CREATE AN AGENDA

I am a strong advocate of structured meetings that allow for discussion. In order to achieve this goal, I will normally send the board a proposed agenda that any board member who wishes to bring up a topic can modify. This is usually done two weeks before the meeting. The week before the meeting, we send out a board package that consists of the final agenda, the minutes of the last board meeting, financials for the quarter, as well as a summary of any resolutions to be discussed and voted on at the meeting. Figure 21-1 offers a sample board agenda.

Of course, the sample agenda can be modified greatly to meet the needs of the organization.

The review of operations by the CFO and CEO should focus on what goals were achieved and those that were missed. It should include a discussion of cash flows and how the company met its cash needs. Various items on the P&L should be discussed, includ-

FIGURE 21-1 ■ Sample Board Agenda.

SAMPLE BOARD AGENDA Date ___/___/___	
1. Open meeting	CEO/Chairman
2. Approve minutes of last meeting	CEO
3. Review operations	
◆ Financials, QTR, and year to date	CFO
◆ Discussion of activities	CEO
4. Significant sales events	VP Sales
5. Other special reports	
◆ Research & development	VP R&D
◆ Legal	CFO
6. Forecast for forthcoming QTR and year as compared with budget	CFO
7. Reports of board committees	
◆ Audit	Audit Chair
◆ Compensation	Compensation Chair
8. New items and resolutions	Sponsor
9. Open discussion	All
10. Closed discussion	Board Only
11. Set date for next meeting	CEO
12. Close meeting	Chair

ing sales and margins. In other words, key operating issues should be clarified. The CEO should discuss any items that are of interest to the board, including problems and successes.

I typically bring in other members of the staff to give special reports on our progress in various areas. For example, if we were involved in a major R&D project, I would have the vice president of R&D present a show-and-tell on the project.

The next typical area of discussion is on the future direction of the company compared to the plan and any action necessary to get there. The chairs of various committees of the board then submit their reports as appropriate. And finally, as part of the formal portion of the meeting, any resolutions are raised and voted on after discussion.

The rest of the meeting is an open discussion with and without management present. It is at this point that new ideas are discussed and the board offers many of its ideas and opinions.

BEFORE THE MEETING

Quite frankly, I really like having the board and management meet the night before the formal meeting to interact informally. I like to have dinner in a private venue somewhere to allow this interaction to take place.

At this informal meeting I often have an informative presentation of the key areas of operations or sales before dinner—again, a show-and-tell that helps inform directors. Another way to stimulate director discussion is by visiting operating locations and taking plant tours so the directors can touch and feel the company first-hand.

SMALL BUSINESSES

If your company is small and you don't want to impose the legal requirements and liabilities of a board on the company, an informal board of advisers may be the way to go.

If you do have a formal board or if your company is public, then directors' and officers' insurance (D&O insurance) is mandatory and very expensive. I really don't know of any director of a public company who would serve without some protection from D&O insurance.

Another alternative exists for small businesses, which is not really a board but provides advice just like a board. It is Vistage®, an international organization of CEOs organized in small groups of 10–20 who meet monthly to discuss business problems and challenges. Their meetings consist of a lecturer who provides a three-hour seminar on a subject like marketing or motivating personnel, followed by a discussion of corporate issues. The group chair also visits each of the members monthly, on a one-to-one basis, to discuss any business-related issues or problems they may have. Vistage is in San Diego but has groups in virtually every city in the United States and in many foreign countries.

Young Presidents Organization (YPO) is another group that acts as a quasi board. It is designed for larger companies and is more social in nature but provides great contact with accomplished leaders in commerce who might be persuaded to offer advice or join your board. A board is only as good as the people who serve on it and how management heeds its advice. A company needs to realize that the board is a resource to be used, not a burden to be tolerated.

CHAPTER TWENTY-TWO

IMPLEMENTATION

In this book I have offered a series of actions that will lead to increased profitability for any size corporation. The greatest frustration for a consultant such as me is to give advice knowing it will yield success, yet watch the client not follow through or implement the suggestions.

I have been fixing and improving companies for over 30 years, and the advice I have given in these pages really works. I have utilized these methods time and time again in real-life situations to fix troubled companies and the results speak for themselves.

In the introduction to this book, I stated that the greatest single management problem was failure to react to changing conditions, or in short "inertia." Another problem is that each of the recommendations I have made requires some effort to implement and certainly discipline to continue using over time. The toughest problem is convincing others that the studies and changes I propose are worth the effort and will work.

I recently assisted a company in identifying a key problem with its sales force. The solution was to add some key personnel immediately through the use of executive search. The company had previously tried some hit-and-miss search methods, but there was a very large fallout rate due to poor initial screening. The cost was going to be high, but I helped negotiate a very low rate considering what we were asking the recruiter to do. Because of cost factors, the CEO decided to return to his old method of search, which we knew was a failure.

The company was bleeding cash and another mistake in judgment would probably kill it. The CEO, I believe, had made that mistake. My failure was in not being able to convince him that my advice was correct and that he should have the courage to follow it.

In the case of the jewelry company in Chapter 5, it took over two years to convince middle management that pricing changes would not only be beneficial but would not erode volume if done correctly. In that instance the CEO was convinced and had the perseverance to push the concept of niche pricing down into the organization so that it would be implemented. The jewelry company recently sold to a buyer for 300 percent more than the stock was worth when we started.

Hedge funds and distressed company purchases depend on this inability of managers to modify their behavior. They step in; provide capital and managers who will solve problems; and end up with a viable, salable company.

I have provided you with a distillation of action steps that can make a company more profitable. It takes a combination of guts, perseverance, and energy to use them, but I am sure that you will be pleased with the results.

INDEX